ACCESS FOR ALL

About the University of Nevada, Reno

Inspired by its land grant foundation, the University of Nevada, Reno serves the economic, social, environmental, and cultural needs of the citizens of Nevada, the nation, and the world (Northwest Accreditation Report 2016).

The University was established in 1864, the year of the state's admission into the Union. Classes were first offered by the University in 1874 in Elko as a preparatory high school. In 1885, the University was moved to Reno, near the center of the state's population (University of Nevada, Reno General Catalog). The 1886 register of the University of Nevada referenced that the State Constitution in Section I of Article XI, declares that, "the Legislature shall encourage by all suitable means the promotion of intellectual, literary, scientific, mining, mechanical, agricultural and moral improvement."

Within the University of Nevada, Reno, twelve schools and colleges offer undergraduate and graduate majors. Graduate-level training and research, including a number of doctoral-level programs, further the University's mission to create scholarly activity. The University is classified by the Carnegie Foundation for the Advancement of Teacher as a Comprehensive Doctoral (institution) with medical and/or veterinary medicine. This designation indicates that the University awards doctoral degrees in the humanities, the social sciences, and in science, technology, engineering, and mathematics (STEM) disciplines as well as medicine. The University also offers professional education in other health professions, business, education, engineering, public policy, and social work (University of Nevada, Reno General Catalog, 2017).

ACCESS
FOR ALL

EXPANDING OPPORTUNITY AND PROGRAMS TO
SUPPORT SUCCESSFUL STUDENT OUTCOMES
AT THE UNIVERSITY OF NEVADA, RENO

Edited by
MELISA N. CHOROSZY, PH.D. *and* THEODOR M. MEEK, MA

UNIVERSITY OF NEVADA PRESS *Reno & Las Vegas*

University of Nevada Press | Reno, Nevada 89557 USA
www.unpress.nevada.edu

LIBRARY OF CONGRESS CATALOGING-IN-PUBLICATION DATA
Names: Choroszy, Melisa N. (Melisa Nancy), 1949- author. | Meek, Theodor M.,
    author.
Title: Access for all : expanding opportunity and programs to support successful
    student outcomes at the University of Nevada, Reno / Melisa N. Choroszy and
    Theodor M. Meek.
Description: Reno ; Las Vegas : University of Nevada Press, [2019] | Identifiers:
    LCCN 2018037841 (print) | LCCN 2018044089 (ebook) | ISBN 9781948908191
    (ebook) | ISBN 9781948908184 (pbk. : alk. paper)
Subjects: LCSH: Low-income college students--Services for--Nevada--Reno--Case
    studies. | First-generation college students--Services for--Nevada--Reno--Case
    studies. | University of Nevada, Reno--Students--Case studies.
Classification: LCC LC4069.6 (ebook) | LCC LC4069.6 .C56 2019 (print) | DDC
    378.1/98269420979355--dc23
LC record available at https://lccn.loc.gov/2018037841

FIRST PRINTING

Manufactured in the United States of America

Contents

Part III: Success After Graduation

Access and Opportunity: Where Did It All Begin?

Throughout this collection, you will find that the University of Nevada, Reno is fiercely committed to serving our diverse student body. While this book focuses specifically on helping income-qualified, first-generation, and ethnically diverse students. This work may also be adapted to serve many other unique groups of students. The university is often described as a place of learning that is "big-enough-to-challenge yet small-enough-to-care," striving to support *all* of Nevada's population. The University seeks to increase the recruitment and graduation of a diverse student body prepared for global agency and citizenship. The individuals on campus who lead these programs and services are devoted to realizing this goal.

This book is divided into three parts. Part One presents the innovative ways in which the University supports developing the college-going culture of its prospects. With programs beginning as early as the sixth grade, the University has committed to reaching down into the educational pipeline to support the success of our students long before they ever step foot on the University's campus as freshmen. Part One has a particular emphasis on developing an understanding of why college is important and how a college degree can sustain one's success. This section focuses on creating relationships with young individuals. Before a student can come to the University and feel welcomed and connected, they must first know about the University and the plentiful opportunities it provides. Through introducing younger students to college students, these relationships are kindled.

Part Two focuses on the resources that support a diverse student body at the University. These programs and services are dynamic and effective. Some are only in their infancy, as young as three years old, while others have been established for more than fifty years. Our programs range from being designed for freshmen to preparing those in their senior years for success after graduation. Through well-developed relationships with faculty, administrators, and staff, these programs contribute to the retention and graduation of our students. Some of our programs were developed from federal grants, while others have been funded as priorities of the president of the University, as well as the chancellor of the Nevada System of Higher Education.

Part Three describes success after graduation. The University provides programs and services to support students through graduate programs and certificates as well as preparedness for moving directly into the world of work. The McNair Scholars Program and the School of Medicine's Post-Baccalaureate Program support students who have an ambition to continue their post-secondary education on to an advanced degree. Further, this part shares our vision of the future of the nation's programs that exist to support our underrepresented, minority students.

This book was written so that we could share our best practices, research, and assessment results with our colleagues in higher education. We are proud of the results of our University's engagement in this important work. We hope that other universities may use the ideas from this book to develop programs of their own that fit their unique circumstances and student populations. We are committed to student success, and we would like to be an inspiration for you to do the same.

Our work is now more significant than ever before. Student success is the key to an educated populace who are able to demonstrate thoughtful and sound reasoning while engaging in civil intellectual discourse. The ability to think critically, to value diverse thoughts and opinions, and to model proficiency in cultural competence are the keys to a peaceful and productive world economy.

We hope that you enjoy this collection and appreciate the excellence that is embedded into the writings of our contributors. This book is merely a snapshot of the extraordinary work being done at this institution. This work is not easy nor complete—and the individuals who have contributed to the effort remain committed to the continuous development to support our students—*each and every one of them.*

PART I

Cultivating the College-Going Culture

The best college planning and preparation is said to begin in the student's formative years of their early education. In actuality, for some students it may seem that college preparation starts on the day of the application deadline. Regardless, one thing is for certain: Any form of preparation for higher education is vital to the success of a student's time in college. Services originating out of higher education must be prepared to support every student, regardless of their level of college preparation. The programs discussed in this section seek to engage students at all age levels, from sixth and seventh grades, to their final year of high school.

CHAPTER 1

The "College Knowledge" Gap

Time to Test Our Assumptions Directly

JENNIFER LOWMAN, PH.D.

Jennifer Lowman, Ph.D. is the director of the Office of Student Persistence Research at the University of Nevada, Reno. Her research background is in the social psychology of educational and occupational pathways. She supports program assessment and conducts original research for the continuous improvement of programs and services on campus.

First-generation college students (FGCS) have less *college knowledge* than continuing-generation students. College knowledge is a dimension of college readiness that captures the awareness and ability to navigate procedures and cultural expectations both *before* (Vargas, 2004) and *after* (Conley, 2008) students enter college. First-generation students have parents who have little information or advice to give, as they did not attend college; furthermore, research shows high school counselors are not good proxies for post-enrollment information (Rosenbaum, 2001; Rueda, 2005). First-generation college students enter college with less college knowledge to such an extent that their adjustment, involvement, academic progress, persistence, and graduation are significantly lower or "at-risk" (Chen, 2005; Choy, 2001; Ishitani, 2003; Rosenbaum, Deil-Amen, & Person, 2006).

College-preparation programs, especially those that are federally funded such as GEAR UP or the TRiO programs (e.g., Talent Search, Upward Bound), provide students the procedural information needed to access college, but not necessarily to graduate from college (Gandara & Bail, 2001; Perna, 2002). Even then, such procedural information is secondary to program goals and activities meant to inspire students to attend college (Perna, 2002). The increase in college aspirations over the last few decades has been substantial, as has enrollment in college, especially community college (Snyder & Dillow, 2016). This may be in no small part due to the efforts of preparation programs. Unfortunately, their impact is difficult to evaluate for a number of methodological and analytical reasons. Although college-preparation programs claim doubling the college-going rate among first-generation, low-income, and underrepresented students, these claims lack evidence and obfuscate details on destinations by college type (two-year or four-year) or enrollment intensity (part-time or full-time) (Gandara & Bail, 2001).

College-preparation programs also attempt to deliver procedural information to parents. Unfortunately, parent involvement in preparation programs is a well-known challenge even in the quarter of programs for which it is mandatory (Perna, 2002; Swail & Perna, 2000). Nonetheless, getting procedural information to parents is paramount, as it may not only increase college access, but persistence as well. For example, college access *and* persistence increased when parents worked one-on-one with a professional on the Free Application for Federal Student Aid (Bettinger et al., 2012), which is widely perceived as one of the biggest bureaucratic hurdles to college access. The mechanism through which this intensive support increased persistence needs more research, especially considering scaling up a program of dedicated professional guidance for each FGCS's family is not realistic.

Once in college, FGCS college knowledge is not assessed at entry or as a condition for access to support programs and resources while enrolled. Failure to directly assess college knowledge creates both programmatic and analytic problems for college-success programs. First, the ubiquitous use of parent education to identify first-generation students maintains an assumption that *all* FGCS have a deficit of college knowledge and this *deficit* explains their relatively poor college outcomes. Second, by extension, the impact of collegiate support programs on FGCS procedural and cultural knowledge is difficult to demonstrate because it is not directly assessed. We need to stop relying on indirect approaches such as parent education for identification and program membership for impact. We need to assess the *gap in college knowledge* assumed to exist and which college-success programs purport to close.

The Problem Relying on Parent Education

The National Center for Education Statistics (NCES) has produced a wealth of information describing the preparation, enrollment, persistence, transfer, and graduation of first-generation students defined as students whose parents never enrolled in a postsecondary certificate or degree program *(see, for example, Choy, 2001 and her review of research based on the NCES longitudinal surveys: NELS, BPS, and B&B national longitudinal surveys)*. The most widely cited research on FGCS outcomes is based on NCES surveys that use this definition, including the oft-cited *Toolbox* studies by Clifford Adelman (1999; 2004; 2006).

It appears that children are not good sources for parental education attainment. Adelman (1999) found that only fifty percent of students correctly identified their parents' level of educational attainment. When accuracy is a concern, it is best to have the parent report their educational attainment as applicants do when they apply for federal financial aid. Moreover, measurement should approximate a continuous scale to identify gradations in the contribution of parental postsecondary experiences to the next generation's educational attainment. For example, there appear to be benefits of having parents with "some college" compared to having parents with no college, which include increased enrollment, persistence, and graduation (Chen, 2005; Choy, 2001).

This brings to light two related issues with current approaches in measurement: (1) Dichotomous indicators, wherein students are labeled either first-generation or not, conceals important differences between students and hides potentially beneficial experiences parents may have had in postsecondary educational settings, perhaps less traditional settings, that did not lead to a certificate or degree; and (2) a reliance on categories of degree completion (e.g., high school completion, associate's degree, bachelor's degree, graduate degree) that may allow for more fine-grained identification of differences, also obscures experiences or paths in postsecondary educational settings that do not lead to a traditional certificate or degree. The positive benefit of some college on student outcomes is an important one to document and understand, but current practices overlook its contribution. As such, it tends to be ignored by practitioners when they make decisions about whom to target for services and outreach.

Overall, parent education is an indirect indicator of the college knowledge we assume students may or may not hold at the time they enter college. Much of the research on which patterns of enrollment, persistence, and graduation is based uses the cutoff point "high school or less" to generate a profile of first-generation student outcomes. It is important to keep in mind that this is a practical and analytical decision made for analyzing and summarizing data. Conceptually, parent education captures exposure to mainstream educational opportunity. Although it is useful to make comparisons of average exposure for different social groups to identify disparities and demand change, we must not lose sight of all the variation around the average or fail to see how different experiences intersect. Essentially, practitioners have to go beyond the conceptual limitations posed by singular indicators to identify the mechanisms through which they can create change and increase educational opportunity. We should continue to examine the influence of parent education but limit its use to research and reporting; we should not continue to use it as a proxy for what is of primary interest to our retention programs and services. We need to identify the needs of students directly and assess our efforts accordingly.

Closing the College Knowledge Gap?

Although there are many measurement challenges, direct assessment will improve our ability to evaluate program impact on the knowledge, values, and behavior of FGCS students, as well as help program coordinators be more intentional in the delivery of college knowledge. The overreliance on parent education level to identify first-generation students hinders our ability to assess program impact because as an identification indicator it is indirectly associated with the deficit of interest. We need to focus directly on the gap in knowledge that impedes college success in order to improve learning, enhance program impact, and increase graduation rates. We have the resources, collaborative culture, and a clear impetus to measure the impact of support programs on graduation. Now we also need to narrow our focus on the treatment that boosts retention. Until we do, our understanding of the impact of support services will remain very limited, and our assessments will offer few recommendations for program improvement.

The best statistical techniques available are correlational, not causal. Unless we directly measure changes in knowledge and behavior, we cannot explain why certain outcomes are more or less likely. For example, a recent GEAR UP evaluation found that Nevada GEAR UP students attending the University of Nevada, Reno persisted to their sophomore year at the same rate as their peers (Sanchez, Lowman, & Hill, 2016). Evidence of the GEAR UP program's impact was indirect at best as no program-level outcomes were included in the evaluation: Such information was simply not available. Even with advanced statistical modeling to control the influence of precollege characteristics and experiences, the results identify patterns only and explain a small portion of the variation in outcomes. That said, it is possible to increase the rigor and diligence of such an evaluation by measuring college knowledge among incoming students and assessing knowledge growth over time or retrospectively. Either method, described below, will help *explain* the patterns observed in retention research and give insight into causal processes underlying student development.

Value-Added assessment methods: A pre-post design is optimal to assess the value certain experiences add to knowledge. Ideally, the initial assessment would take place before students are exposed to campus services or programs; during or soon after admission, for example. All incoming students should be assessed to identify the base of knowledge for the incoming class, as well as special groups of interest such as FGCS. Next, the initial assessment of college knowledge could be used to target students in most need of support. Similarly, the initial assessment would provide programs a baseline of college knowledge from which to develop learning opportunities. Finally, FGCS learning outcomes and programmatic outcomes could be compared to nonparticipating FGCS students and continuing-generation students as well. Evidence of program impact would then be derived from both internal assessments (e.g., learning outcomes of participants, knowledge gains) and external comparisons to nonparticipant student groups.

Retrospective assessment methods: Retrospective assessments have been found to have comparable validity (i.e., accuracy) and reliability (i.e., consistency) for measurement of subjective experiences of program-related change (Hill & Betz, 2005; Howard et al., 1979; Lam

& Bengo, 2003). To prompt students to rank and rate experiences in hindsight, instructions and questions need to be carefully worded to minimize cognitive biases to which retrospective accounts are susceptible (e.g., social desirability bias, positivity bias, correspondence bias). Retrospective assessments facilitate a more subjective account of learning, but they are no less of a direct evaluation of program outcomes. Retrospective assessments are best suited for the evaluation of learning outcomes that result from a recent experience in a program or service. They are less well-suited to the assessment of knowledge gains as time from the experience extends.

Conclusions

From a societal perspective, increasing access to college does little good if FGCS students do not get to reap the rewards of a college degree. The research is quite clear regarding the benefit of a bachelor's degree for access to social mobility (Choy, 2001). Survey data from the Beginning Postsecondary Study revealed that first-generation status represents an acute disadvantage towards completing a degree in five years (13 versus 33 percent) or leaving without a degree (45 versus 29 percent) (Choy, 2001). However, bachelor's degree attainment appeared to level the playing field. First-generation college students who completed a bachelor's degree were just as likely to earn a job with a comparable salary when compared to continuing-generation bachelor degree recipients (Choy, 2001; Nunez & Cuccaro-Alamin, 1998). Likewise, three years postgraduation, salary parity remained between first-generation and continuing-generation graduates (Horn & Zahn, 2001).

Going forward we need to directly identify the college knowledge that first-generation, low-income, and underrepresented students lack and target their needs explicitly. The primary benefit of this approach will be an increase both in the rigor of services and programs, as well as an opportunity to fully assess the impact of supplemental information and its delivery. A secondary benefit will be the identification of evidence-based practices that can be scaled up to increase the persistence and graduation of students not directly served. Essentially, an approach that benefits FGCS is more likely to benefit the general population than is an approach based on the needs of the general population

(Arnold, Lu, & Armstrong, 2012; Conley, 2008). More rigorous assessment can help identify the college knowledge students need to succeed. More rigorous assessment can help identify bureaucratic and cultural hurdles that arise when students encounter the sheer size of our institution and its rapidly changing composition. Finally, more rigorous assessment can lift the burden of navigating college off the shoulders of students and promote access to the core learning opportunities our institution provides.

References

Adelman, C. (1999). Answers in the tool box: Academic intensity, attendance patterns, and *bachelor's degree attainment*. Washington, DC: U.S. Department of Education.

Adelman, C. (2004). *Principal indicators of student academic histories in postsecondary education, 1972–2000*. Washington, DC: U.S. Department of Education, Institute of Education Sciences.

Adelman, C. (2006). *The toolbox revisited: Paths to degree Completions from High school through college*. Washington, DC: U.S. Department of Education.

Arnold, K. D., Lu, E. C., & Armstrong, K. J. (2012). The ecology of college readiness. *ASHE Higher Education Report*, 38(5), 91–107.

Bettinger, E. P., Long, B., Oreopoulos, P., & Sanbonmatsu, L. (2012). The role of application assistance and information in college decisions. *Quarterly Journal of Economics*, 127, 3, 1205–1242.

Cabrera, A. F., Prabhu, R., Deil-Amen, R., Terenzini, P., Lee, C. & Franklin, R. (2006). Increasing the preparedness of at-risk students. *Journal of Latinos & Education*, 5(2),79–97.

Chen, X. (2005). *First-Generation Students in Postsecondary Education: A Look at their College Transcripts*. Washington, DC: National Center for Education Statistics.

Choy, S. (2001). Students Whose Parents Did Not Go to College: Postsecondary Access, Persistence, and Attainment. Washington, DC: National Center for Education Statistics.

Conley, D. T. (2008). Rethinking college readiness. *New Directions for Higher Education*, 144, 3–13. DOI: 10.1002/he.321

Gándara, P., & Bial, D. (2001). *Paving the way to postsecondary education: K-12 intervention programs for underrepresented youth*. Washington, DC: U.S. Department of Education, National Center for Educational Statistics, Office of Educational Research and Improvement.

Hill, L. G., & Betz, D. I. (2005). Revisiting the retrospective pretest. *American Journal of Evaluation*, 26(4), 501–517.

Howard, G. S., Ralph, K. M., Gulanick, N. A., Maxwell, S. E., Nance, D. W., & Gerber,

S. K. (1979). Internal invalidity in pretest-postest self-report evaluations and a re-evaluation of retrospective pretests. *Applied Psychological Measurement, 3*, 1–23.

Ishitani, T. T. (2003). *A Longitudinal Approach to Assessing Attrition Behavior among First-generation Students: Time-varying Effects of Pre-college Characteristics. Research in Higher Education*, 44(4): 433–449.

Lam, T. C. M., & Bengo, P. (2003). A comparison of three retrospective self-reporting methods of measuring change in instructional practice. *American Journal of Evaluation,* 24(1), 65–80.

Nunez, A. & S. Cuccaro-Alamin. (1998). *First-Generation Students: Undergraduates whose parents never enrolled in postsecondary education*. Washington, DC: National Center for Education Statistics.

Perna, L. W. (2002). Precollege outreach programs: Characteristics of programs serving historically underrepresented groups of students. *Journal of College Student Development*, 43, 64–83.

Rosenbaum, J. E. (2001). *Beyond college for all: Career paths for the forgotten half.* New York: Russell Sage.

Rosenbaum, J. E., Deil-Amen, R. & Person, A. E. (2006). *After Admission. From college access to college success.* New York: Russell Sage.

Rueda, R. (2005). Making sense of what we know: From nine propositions to future research and interventions. In W. G. Tierney, Z. B. Corwin, and J. E. Colyar (Eds.), *Preparing for college: Nine elements of effective outreach* (pp. 189–200). Albany, NY: SUNY Press.

Sanchez, J., Lowman, J. L., & Hill, K. (2016). Performance and persistence outcomes of GEAR Up students: Leveling the playing field in higher education. *Journal of College Student Retention: Research, Theory, & Practice.*

Snyder, T. D., de Brey, C., and Dillow, S. A. (2016). *Digest of Education Statistics 2015* (NCES 2016-014). National Center for Education Statistics, Institute of Education Sciences, U.S. Department of Education. Washington, DC.

Swail, W. S., &Perna, L. W. (2000). *A View of the Landscape: Results of the National Survey of Outreach Programs*. In *Outreach Program Handbook 2001*. New York: The College Board.

Vargas, J. H. (2004). *College knowledge: Addressing information barriers to college*. Boston, MA.: The Education Resources Institute (TERI)

CHAPTER 2

Dean's Future Scholars

Lessons Learned in the Evolution of a Precollegiate Outreach Program Based in an Academic College

PAT MILTENBERGER, PH.D., JAMES BEATTIE, PH.D., and MATT SMITH, PH.D.

Pat Miltenberger is the former vice-president of student services and emeritus professor of higher education leadership at the University of Nevada, Reno. Her career spanned more than forty years at both the community college and university level. She began her career as an Upward Bound director, which influenced her commitment and work with first-generation low-income students.

James Beattie is an associate director in the Center for Student Engagement at the University of Nevada, Reno advising and guiding student government officers in responsible servant leadership. He returned to school to pursue a master in sociology and a Ph.D. in Educational Leadership after a successful, yet unfulfilling career in the private sector. He found his passion in higher education while developing and implementing a mentoring program for first-generation and low-income college students. His research interests include successful characteristics of academic outreach programs, college access, retention, and graduation for underrepresented students, as well as organizational theory.

Matt Smith is the director of the Center for Academic Support and Achievement (CASA) and the Center for Multi-Ethnic and Cultural Affairs (MECA) at Tacoma Community College (WA) serving underrepresented students through intrusive advising, mentoring, and resource referrals. His research interests include persistence and success of first-generation students of color, and the dynamics of ethnicity at Historically Black Colleges and Universities. Smith holds a Ph.D. in educational leadership from the University of Nevada, Reno and both a bachelor of arts in music and a master's in teaching from Hampton University (VA).

Colleges and universities have a long history of attempting to attract, retain, and graduate underrepresented students through precollegiate outreach programs (Gullatt, V. & Jan, W., 2003). The evolution of precollegiate outreach programs is commonly attributed to the establishment of the Upward Bound (UB) program in 1964 as part of the Economic Opportunity Act. Additional federal programs targeting access and retention of first-generation/low-income (FGLI) students were established under the 1965 Higher Education Act and its subsequent reauthorizations, including the Talent Search, Student Support Services, McNair Scholars, GEAR UP, and Title IV Federal Financial Aid programs. The first three of these programs, UB, Talent Search, and Student Support Services (originally called Special Services for Disadvantaged Students) became known as TRiO, and the name is still in use today (COE, n.d.). These programs have endured despite criticism questioning their effectiveness and success as well as whether such program administration is an appropriate role of the federal government.

Some UB evaluation studies have indicated that participants were up to four times more likely to earn an undergraduate degree than students with a similar background not in a TRiO program (Fields, 2001). Other studies on Upward Bound's effectiveness have been mixed. A Cahalan (2009) study found that while the program was effective in enrolling students in postsecondary education, it was not as effective in graduating them. The longevity of Upward Bound and its perceived success have spawned many institutional initiatives for precollegiate programs. The University of Nevada, Reno (UNR) was an early adopter of the Upward Bound program. The first subgrant was awarded in 1966 for a statewide program serving seventy-five students with students attending their first summer session in 1967. The original UB program at UNR was focused on black students in the urban Las Vegas area and Native American students in Nevada's rural colonies and reservations. The University was also awarded a Talent Search subgrant in 1966. Subsequently in 1967, the University of Nevada, Las Vegas (UNLV) was awarded an Upward Bound grant. The UNR program then shifted its focus to Northern Nevada. Upward Bound regulations have evolved over the years but generally enroll students who have completed eighth grade, are low income based on federal criteria, and demonstrate potential for college. Today the University administers three Upward Bound subgrants as well as the McNair Scholars Program, Student Support Services, and GEAR UP.

The forces driving the development of precollegiate outreach at UNR were not unique to Nevada. During the late 1950s and early '60s the University's enrollment of Native American and black students was minimal. Warren d'Azevedo's 1975 publication *American Indian and Black Students at the University of Nevada, Reno 1874–1974* noted that "open and flagrant discrimination was practiced throughout Nevada against all ethnic minorities, but with particular viciousness against Black Americans" (p. 3). Native American students suffered similar discrimination and were often forbidden to attend schools within their community or were forced to attend Bureau of Indian Affairs or out-of-state schools (d'Azevedo, 1975). By 1960 it was believed only three black students and one Native American student had graduated from the University since its opening in 1874.

Support for black students and civil rights became a campus issue in the mid-1960s. Several negative incidents were publicized regarding black students' experiences of racism both on and off campus. Members of the Faculty Senate demanded greater attention to discrimination issues both on campus and in the local community. Black student-athletes were the most visible and vocal minority on campus at that time. Student clubs and organizations addressing ethnic student interests began to surface, and the campus newspaper took on a key role in both perpetuating and condemning discrimination (d'Azevedo, 1975). Students and faculty began to call for a greater commitment to the recruitment and outreach to communities of color. At that time UB and the Talent Search subgrant (which had moved from UNR to the Inter-Tribal Council of Nevada) were the only programs addressing low-income and/or minority student outreach. In 1969, after a series of student-led confrontations and community meetings, the president of UNR established the first locally funded outreach initiative, the Educational Opportunities Program (EOP, not to be confused with the federal program of the same name). The program hired a part-time director and reorganized an endowment to provide fifty scholarships for minority students. The University had grant-in-aids (fee waivers) in place for Native American students as well as the Fleischmann Indian Scholarship program. Although the EOP program was met with criticism for its primary focus on black students, it became the precursor to other campus-based efforts to recruit and retain students of color.

Changing Demographics and a Changing Nevada

From the controversies of the sixties and early seventies to today, Nevada demographics tell an important story. In 1970 ninety-one percent of Nevadans were white, by the year 2000 that figure had dropped to seventy-five percent, and by 2010 sixty-six percent of Nevadans were white. The fastest-growing populations are Hispanics and Asians. During this same period, the Las Vegas metropolitan area became one of the fastest-growing areas in the nation. In 2000, the two most populated counties were quickly approaching no ethnic majority in the K-12 public school system.

Both UNR and UNLV had over these same years developed sophisticated campus-based student outreach efforts to recruit and retain students of color as well as the majority of the federal TRiO programs. UNR opened a recruitment office in the Las Vegas area in 1991. Both universities participated in a number of federal and state initiatives aimed at improving the high school graduation and college-going rates. Nevada had consistently received an F in participation and completion rates (Measuring Up, 2008).

In 1998, the University of Nevada, Reno hired a new dean of the College of Education. The dean noted the disparity between the lack of diversity of the K-12 teaching workforce and the changing student population. The demographics were striking. Nevada had moved from a predominately rural white state to a state with two highly concentrated multicultural urban populations. In an attempt to address the lack of diversity in the northern school districts, the dean emulated a program he had observed at Texas Tech University. The dean envisioned the precollegiate outreach program at UNR as an opportunity to bring diverse students to campus, inform these potential students about the College of Education, and recruit more diverse students to the profession of teaching. The program at Texas Tech involved bringing public school students together a few times a year for one-day conferences. According to the dean, the purpose was to imprint the idea that "You can go to college, you can go to UNR, and you can become a teacher" (Beattie, 2013).

The dean garnered support across campus by showing a video of the Texas Tech program to University administrators and faculty leaders. These early contacts provided a launching pad for creating interest and awareness of the program's intent. Of particular interest was the idea of bringing students to a campus in the sixth grade rather than waiting until they were high school age. In December 2000, the dean received a $5,000 donation from a local teacher's mother who learned about the program. The donation provided the seed money to bring students to campus for the first conference. Later, the dean set aside funds for a graduate assistant to recruit five sixth-grade students from 10 Title I schools in the Washoe County School District to establish the first cohort of Dean's Future Scholars (DFS). The sixth-grade teachers and the school counselor were asked to recommend students. The major criteria was that the students be low income and potentially the first in their family to go to college.

Following the program's inception in 2000, DFS evolved into six major components based on college outreach research, faculty scholarship, and funding opportunities. The program components eventually included: middle school enrichment (2002); school year mentoring (2004); summer math credits (2004); a summer bridge program for college credit (2006); summer internships (2006); and a safe place referred to as the lounge (2007). These components moved the program from simply being a booster program (i.e., "you can go to college") to a long-term relationship with the students to provide the skills and direct assistance needed to graduate from high school, enter college, and graduate (Orr, Alcantara, Frazier, Kalinka, & Kaplan, 2007).

The original three-week middle school enrichment program brought students to campus for both cultural enrichment and recreational activities. The intent was to introduce students to the campus and establish bonds between staff and students and create student-to-student peer networks with similar academic goals outside of their neighborhoods (Tinto, 1975 & 1993). The mentoring component was added in 2002 to provide a year-round presence with students at their schools. College students with a similar background as the students were hired, along with several graduate students, to provide on-site school mentoring and assist students with attendance, homework, course scheduling, and adjustment issues. Mentors supported school counselors and became another voice encouraging academic performance to enable college access. In subsequent years, the program began to hire former DFS students, then in college, to mentor the new youth entering the program; this became known as the grow your own model. Eventually, this included hiring DFS graduate students to mentor college students, train, and supervise mentors, and run the day-to-day operations of the program.

In 2004 the summer math component was added to ensure students completed four years of high school math before entering college. Research by Clifford Adelman, United States Department of Education (1999, 2006) indicated that students who completed Algebra II and at least one additional math course in high school were more likely to enter and complete college. The program director discovered that several middle schools were not encouraging or even offering algebra in the eighth grade. The director then pursued and received a private foundation grant to offer the summer math component. DFS students, based on their current math skill level, were enrolled in intensive math courses during the summer for high school credit. The program ran five days per week for six weeks; each day included four hours of instruction and four hours of tutoring (provided by DFS college mentors) as well as math homework. Local school district mathematics teachers taught the course as a part of the regular school district summer school.

In 2006, a summer internship component was added. The director noted that DFS student families had often expressed concern that their students needed to work rather than take time to attend the summer program. The director realized these were legitimate financial concerns for the family and students, and leveraged a federal Workforce Investment Act grant to create paid internships to employ students for eight weeks during the summer of their junior and senior years.

Participants worked four hours a day, four days per week in various jobs across the UNR campus. Students were then able to take college courses in conjunction with their internships. The summer internship component was intended to help program participants develop the skills necessary for successful employment, familiarize them to campus offices and services, and assist them with successful integration into campus life while meeting financial needs (Astin, 1975; Tinto, 1993). An unexpected consequence of the summer internship component was the overwhelmingly positive response to program participants from campus supervisors; faculty and staff in the departments where the students worked frequently hired them as student employees when they enrolled in college their freshman year. In the 2010 cohort of DFS, seventeen of eighteen students who were asked to participate in his case study were offered student employee positions on campus as they began their freshman year, James Beattie's dissertation (2013) noted. Students said that this experience gave them a greater connection to the campus as well as knowledge regarding campus services and programs.

The summer bridge component was developed alongside the summer internship program in 2006. The director realized that because college courses could be utilized as workforce training, student enrollment costs were covered under the Workforce Investment Act. As such, the director used Adelman's (2006) research to seek funding for an eight-week summer bridge program for college credit during the summers of the students' junior and senior years. Students who placed into developmental math and English courses (remedial) were offered the developmental sequence to assure they were at the collegiate level by the fall semester of their freshman year. Other students were enrolled in the required math, English, and social science courses required by the University's core curriculum. Summer bridge also included a first-year experience course designed to support students through the often-difficult transition into college. The course explored a variety of college and life skills such as career opportunities, the Myers-Briggs Type Indicator, technical writing and formatting, transfer articulation, financial literacy, time management, study habits, campus and community resources, and group work. This advanced first-year experience course for newly admitted freshmen was designed to introduce students to the general resources and expectations of college and encouraged students to become engaged on campus in a variety of ways that research indicates leads to college retention and success (Tinto, 1975, 1993, 2010). This class was made up entirely of DFS students and taught by DFS staff. As such, an unintended consequence was that students indicated the class was a safe space where they could learn what it was like to be a college student without fear of judgment (Beattie, 2013).

The final component of the DFS program was its function as a "Safe Space" at the University. A dedicated space in the College of Education provided staff offices, a lounge with computers and printers, and couches and study tables, as well as a food storage and preparation area. This "Safe Space" was frequently mentioned by students as a place they felt comfortable, safe to "be themselves," away from the usual pressures of being college students. Because the lounge also served as the office for mentors and program staff, students were familiar with the space from their middle school years on. This familiarity contributed to the sense of DFS space on campus as "their" space.

In the 2012–2013 academic year a study was conducted on the 2010 incoming freshman cohort to determine the impact of the six separate components on college student retention through the second semester of their sophomore year. This particular class was selected for the study as they were the first cohort to receive all six programmatic components, as well as continued support throughout college. In the 2003–2004 school year fifty-three students were originally selected for enrollment in the DFS program, of which forty-eight graduated high school. According to the Education State Rankings (2009–2010), Nevada was ranked forty-eighth in the nation, with a graduation rate of 55.8 percent, while the DFS program graduated 90.5 percent of the students they had selected in the sixth grade. Of these forty-eight students twenty-four students matriculated to the University of Nevada, Reno. However, two of those students transferred to Truckee Meadows Community College (TMCC), the local community college, after their first semester; reliable contact information could not be obtained for two students; one student opted to leave for the military (and has since returned to the University); and one student dropped out (Beattie, 2013).

The eighteen remaining students were chosen for the study because they were the only students to receive all of the DFS support services, including a safe space on campus and continued mentoring throughout their college careers. Of those eighteen students, fourteen have graduated, and of those fourteen graduates six have obtained a master's degree and one is pursuing a master's degree. Additionally, one graduate was an engineering major and one was a nursing major, and both have indicated they plan to work for several years and then move on to pursue a graduate degree. Of the remaining four, one enlisted in the military and returned to earn an associate's degree and is pursuing a bachelor's degree; one student dropped out and no longer had reliable contact information; and two students no longer had reliable contact information and could not be reached to determine graduation status. Survey results indicated that each of the six program components aided in the academic success of these DFS students. The underlying theme was that DFS created a family and as such created a platform that was conducive to the reproduction of the necessary social and cultural capital for college entrance, persistence, and graduation (Beattie, 2013). In his Theory of Individual Departure, Tinto (1975, 1993) describes three stages necessary for college integration. Findings of Beattie (2013) indicated that the DFS program provided students the opportunity to experience all three stages, with the exception that DFS students did not separate from past communities. Instead, they created an additional community referred to as family without the necessity of sacrificing who they were outside of the university.

Findings further indicated that the summer middle school enrichment program built strong relationships beginning in the sixth grade with DFS faculty, mentors, and peer groups in a fun and safe atmosphere and they developed an expectation that their summers would be spent at DFS. One student wrote, "It was nice to bond with all of the other kids in my cohort." Another student indicated, "After the middle school program, I looked forward to seeing the same DFS kids every summer, even if the summer classes [summer math component] were a drag."

Findings also indicated that the school-year mentoring program was the cornerstone of the DFS program and served to build long lasting relationships that increased in intensity over time. Students indicated that DFS mentors became like family and they could interact freely with them without fear of judgment. One student wrote, "I loved my DFS mentors. I feel like I grew up with them, and now they're my friends in college." Although many students referred to their mentors as friends, students often referred to their mentors as family. One student said, "They are the second set of siblings because you connect with the mentors on different types of levels." Another student reflected, "They want what is best for us...they are another family." Students indicated that they felt they could always go to DFS mentors for academic or life issues as they felt they had similar goals and experiences. "Mentors were the only people in my life who NEVER put me down and were always a positive influence on my life." Another student reflected on his or her mentor by stating, "He was someone I could go to talk to about anything with, and I was never once judged around [by] him." A third student indicated, "They are all supportive and are willing to help you succeed in your goals." The student reflected on their mentor and wrote, "He was the older brother I never had. He was able to relate to the struggles I had been through; he was always willing to listen and easily start a conversation right on the spot."

Students expressed that the summer math component helped them grow and understand that sacrifice was necessary to get ahead. They began to realize that giving up their summers contributed to their academic success and helped move them ahead of their friends. "It was nice to get ahead of other high school students, but it was also sometimes inconvenient because we never really got a summer vacation." Another student reflected, "It was difficult focusing for hours at a time with just a fifteen-minute break, but it paid off, and it definitely helped me maintain a high GPA in high school." A third student wrote, "At first you are reeled in by the fun games and trips, then they slam you with summer classes. But once you get into the classes and doing the work, it is not bad and it helps you get in higher classes and finish more quickly."

Students also indicated that working with their mentors for tutoring created a safe atmosphere and contributed to their continued success. For example, one student wrote, "It was great to have mentors sit in class with us and tutor us every morning so that we fully understood what was being taught, especially since summer school covers materials so quickly." Another student stated, "It was such a help to have mentors in the morning for tutoring sessions. I took math for three summers in DFS and received nothing below an A." A third student reflected, "Math class became easier for me because of all the help I could get before and after classes." A fourth student wrote, "Tutoring helped a lot, especially with harder math courses and there was always someone to help who knew what they were doing." Students indicated that the summer internship program helped not only to develop work skills, but also to create peer and faculty networks as well. One student reflected on his/her internship and wrote, "It helped me with etiquette and helped me become more professional," while another student reported that the staff of the organization where his/her internship took place helped to develop "skills that are looked at by employers in the real world." One student mentioned that the experience helped to broaden his or her social circle on campus, "I met a lot of college students outside the Dean's Future Scholars program." Another student said, "My managers were the best, and my last summer job [DFS summer Internship placement] after graduating [high school] actually hired me for the semester. It was the best feeling ever."

Findings indicated that the college bridge program helped students in a variety of ways. Students reported very positive experiences with the college bridge component. One student wrote, "I was extremely thankful that I got a chance to get a head start on college courses." Another student wrote, "I got to take actual college courses... It was a rewarding experience that helped prepare me for college." A third student noted, "It was very beneficial in that we already had an idea of what to expect once entering college."

Many students reported perceptions of college readiness. For example, one student reported, "It was a rewarding experience that definitely helped prepare me for college." A second student reflected, "We got to learn how college worked before we actually attended college." Another student wrote, "It was great getting to know the resources on campus... and getting to have a little bit more freedom before being thrown into campus life." A fourth student wrote, "I knew what was expected from a college student and when I entered in the fall, it was like home." A fifth student reflected, "The experience was like the real thing…taking real college classes with real college students and real college professors was mind blowing, yet it prepared us."

As mentioned earlier, an unintended consequence of DFS students taking these courses as a group was the alleviation of some nervousness about college entrance. For example, one student expressed the comfort of attending classes with fellow DFS students and said it "took some of the nervousness and scared feelings away." Another student summarized it by writing, "If it wasn't for this program, my perspective going into college would be totally different. I felt prepared and that there was nothing to be afraid of." One student directly expressed how feeling prepared for college led to comfort and wrote:

"It was a little scary at first. It did end up teaching me that no matter what age you are and no matter what class you are taking, college or not, all you need to do is dedicate yourself and everything will be okay. It really made me less scared to go to college."

Overall, findings indicated that the six program components built upon one another to create a program conducive for successful college entrance, retention, and graduation. Tinto (1993) argued that it was beneficial for students to engage in "anticipatory socialization" or preparation of integration into the college social system prior to entering college (p. 98). Findings indicated that the DFS program appeared to provide a wide array of pathways including mentoring, summer programs, and the lounge for transition. The bridge and summer internship components appeared to address anticipatory socialization by exposing students to the expected norms and beliefs, as well as, behavioral and intellectual patterns before entering college. Student responses indicated that students viewed these relationships as a DFS community. The DFS community seemed to be an integral part of the transition between high school and college and contributed to the acquisition of the necessary social and intellectual skills through social and cultural capital.

Tinto's (1993) theory indicated a need for student engagement with various organizations across campus that included fraternities, sororities, intramural sports, clubs and organizations, student government, extracurricular programs, and working on campus. The DFS program appeared to provide three pathways that facilitated student engagement on campus. First, the lounge appeared to provide a "safe space" or second home where students could eat, sleep, seek help, study, and interact with DFS students and staff in a variety of ways. Second, an unexpected consequence of the summer internship component was that most of the students in the cohort were offered student employment positions through their internships just prior to full-time college entrance (Beattie, 2013). Thus, they began their college careers with the opportunity for on-campus student employment. Finally, through the summer bridge component, students were encouraged to explore various campus clubs and organizations as well as use a variety of campus resources such as: Academic Advising, the Writing Center, the Tutoring Center, the Math Center, and the Knowledge Center.

Findings from this case suggested that all five components may have contributed individually to program participant persistence. However, findings also indicated that program components built upon one another sequentially and increased in intensity over time to contribute to the success of this cohort.

Lessons Learned from the Evolution of the Dean's Future Scholars Program

1. The benefit of being located in an academic college, in this case, the College of Education, enabled the program to take advantage of faculty knowledge and research. Faculty demonstrated an interest in the program, encouraged graduate students to conduct research on the program, and provided assistance in finding funding resources. The dean had a vested interest in the success of the program and was instrumental in obtaining private donations and grants. This college-specific support may not be as present in a precollegiate outreach program housed elsewhere, such as a student services division. Although the outreach program did encourage teaching as a profession, students tended to select majors across disciplines; thus the program was successful for college entrance and retention, less so for creating a pipeline to education-specific majors.

2. Two doctoral dissertation studies of the DFS program found that "relationships matter" (Beattie, 2013; Smith, 2012). Students and staff experienced long-term relationships with the program. In

recent years, staff members were either former mentors or mentees of the program. Mentors believed the program made them better college students, and in some instances the mentors changed their majors to helping professions so they could continue working with youth (Serra, unpublished McNair Scholars project). Unexpectedly, as the DFS students graduated from their undergraduate degree, several entered graduate school and became graduate assistants for the program. As these students have completed their graduate degrees, many are employed in student services, including advising, recruitment, and retention, at the local community colleges, the University, and private colleges.

3. The DFS program evolved from a booster program to a true bridge to college and career. A critical element was flexibility and willingness to change. The dean gave latitude to the staff to pursue funding opportunities and actively sought funding for the program. The program staff listened to parent and student concerns and added components to improve services. The program staff met regularly to discuss student needs and interests and provided training and support for the mentors. The staff and mentors established close ties with school district personnel to assure continued access to students during school hours. The second program director developed an extensive database on the students and the outcomes of the program. This database has served as an important mechanism for finding new funding and continued support from the University.

In 2013, *The Chronicle of Higher Education* published an article on the "Ten Best Practices for Serving First-Generation Students" (Doubleday, 2013). The report was based on the experiences of fifty colleges as a part of the Council of Independent Colleges with underwriting from the Walmart Foundation. The practices identified were: (1) Identify, actively recruit, and continually track first-generation students; (2) bring them to the campus early; (3) focus on the distinctive features of first-generation students; (4) develop a variety of programs that meet students' continuing needs; (5) use mentors; (6) institutionalize a commitment to first-generation students; (7) build community, promote engagement, and make it fun; (8) involve families (but keep expectations realistic); (9) acknowledge, and ease when possible, financial pressures; (10) keep track of your success and failures—what works and what does not.

Through its evolution, the Dean's Future Scholars program clearly met each of the ten best practices. The advantage of being part of an academic college has been evident. A specific college provides an environment that engages faculty and provides research opportunities for graduate students. The support of a dean and the development officer of the college enable greater fundraising opportunities and access to grants. The dedicated physical space for the program can enable a "safe place" for students and mentors. Finally, the graduate school opportunities for students are enhanced by the program's connection to an academic college, its graduate students, and faculty.

References

Adelman, C. (1999). *Answers in the tool box: Academic intensity, attendance patterns, and bachelor's degree attainment.* Washington, DC: U.S. Department of Education.

Adelman, C. (2006). *The toolbox revisited: Paths to degree completion from high school through college.* Washington, DC: U.S. Department of Education.

Astin, A. W. (1975). *Preventing students from dropping out.* San Francisco: Jossey-Bass.

Beattie, J. (2013). *A case study of college persistence for the Dean's Future Scholars program.* (Doctoral Dissertation). Retrieved from ProQuest Dissertations and Theses database. (UMI No. 3595626).

Cahalan, M. (2009). *National evaluation of Upward Bound: Do the conclusions change?* Washington, DC: Council for Opportunity in Education.

Callan, P. (2008). *Measuring up 2008: The national report card of higher education.* San Jose, CA: National Center for Public Policy and Higher Education.

Council for Opportunity in Education (n.d.). TRiO history. Retrieved from http://www.coenet.us/coe_prod_imis/COE/TRiO/History/COE/NAV_TRiO/TRiO_History.aspx?hkey=89b3a80a-3a9e-4580-9fda-38156b9318f8.

d'Azevedo, W. (1975). *American Indian and Black students at the University of Nevada, Reno: 1874–1975.* Reno: University of Nevada, Reno Department of Anthropology.

Doubleday, J. (2013, October 24). 10 'best practices' for serving first-generation students. *Chronicle of Higher Education.* Retrieved from https://www.chronicle.com/article/10-Best-Practices-for/142595.

Fields, C. D. (December 6, 2001). Can TRiO and GEAR-UP continue to co-exist? *Black Issues in Higher Education, 8*(21), 26–31.

Gullatt, Y., & Jan, W. (2003). *How do precollegiate academic outreach programs impact college-going among underrepresented students?* Boston, MA: Pathways to College Network.

Orr, M.J., Alcantara, L., Frazier, F., Kalinka, C.J., & Kaplan, S. (2007). *Boosters, brokers and bridges: Real world ideas for college access programs.* Indianapolis, IN: Lumina Foundation.

Smith, M. (2012). *Mentoring and mental models: Outreach to first-generation, low-income students.* (Doctoral Dissertation). Retrieved from ProQuest Dissertations and Theses database. (UMI No. 3550285).

Tinto, V. (1975). Dropouts from higher education: A theoretical synthesis of recent literature. *A Review of Educational Research, 45,* 89–125.

Tinto, V., (1982). Limits of theory and practice in student attrition. *Journal of Higher Education, 53*(6), 687–700.

Tinto, V. (1993). *Leaving college: Rethinking the causes and cures of student attrition* (2nd ed.). Chicago: University of Chicago Press.

Tinto, V. (2010). *Completing college: Rethinking institutional action.* Chicago: University of Chicago Press.

CHAPTER 3

Upward Bound Today

ELLEN HOUSTON, MA

Ellen Houston is director of the Upward Bound Programs at the University of Nevada, Reno. She supervises three federal grants that prepare first-generation, income-qualified high school students for college. Previously, she served as assistant director in the University's Center for Student Cultural Diversity. She has been a higher education professional for twenty years.

Upward Bound, the first federally funded program in the United States to prepare low-income, first-generation (LIFG) students for postsecondary education, emerged from the Economic Opportunity Act of 1964 as a key element of President Lyndon B. Johnson's War on Poverty (U.S. Department of Education, 2014). Since that time, Upward Bound has motivated and tutored millions of low-income students from families in which neither parent holds a college degree, helping the students move from poverty to the middle class.

There are three different types of Upward Bound programs: the classic Upward Bound model, which is designed to assist students in the successful matriculation and graduation from postsecondary education; Upward Bound Math Science, which strengthens the math and science skills of participants in order to prepare them to excel in STEM majors and career fields; and Veterans Upward Bound, which assists U.S. military veterans to gain the academic and other requisite skills necessary for the successful transition to postsecondary education (U.S. Department of Education, 2014). All three types of Upward Bound programs provide free, structured college preparation to students who live at or below 150 percent of the federal poverty level, where their chances of earning a bachelor's degree are nearly nine times less than those of their peers in the top family-income bracket (U.S. Department of Education, 2014). Despite enormous challenges unique to a low-income environment, Upward Bound participants are three times more likely to complete a college degree in six years than those who did not participate in college access services, according to a 2015 report from the Pell Institute, a nonprofit educational research organization.

Thanks to its long and rich history, the Upward Bound programs of today have developed into a complex mix of both old and new. Program participants are still receiving many of the same services as their 1967 counterparts: one-on-one academic advising, tutoring, summer programs designed to prepare them for academic success in the coming year of high school, educational and cultural field trips, and assistance with college applications, as well as financial aid and scholarships. Yet the methods by which those services are delivered and assessed have rapidly changed to keep abreast of federal regulations, technological advances, and modern pedagogy. As professionals in the oldest educational equity programs in existence, Upward Bound staff members must keep sight of the programs' social justice mission and remain true to best practices that have come from fifty years of working with first-generation, income-qualified students (Galvez & Houston, 2016). However, in our rapidly changing global society of our current world, Upward Bound professionals must also prepare our students to be innovators and leaders who are a force for change (Galvez & Houston, 2016). That is the critical role of Upward Bound today.

Access inequality in the United States continues to be evidenced by the growing disparity in graduation rates between the rich and the poor, making the need for educational-equity programs such as Upward Bound as great as ever. According to a 2015 Pell Institute report, only 74 percent of students with families in America's bottom income quartile (less than $34,933 annually) graduate high school as compared to 90 percent of their peers in the highest income quartile. Of those low-income graduates, only 44 percent enroll in postsecondary education, while 77 percent of highest income quartile students continue on to college (Pell Institute, 2015). Further, low-income, first-generation (LIFG) students have a six-year completion rate at four-year institutions of 31.6 percent compared to 71.2 percent for their non-LIFG counterparts (Mortensen, 2016). The six-year bachelor's degree completion rates for students increase with every $10,000 more of parental income, which explains why the difference in graduation rates between students from families with $125,000–$149,000 in annual income and those with $0–$9,000 in annual income is more than 40 percent (Mortensen, 2016).

This inequality based on income is especially troubling given that the buying power of the federal Pell Grant is steadily dropping. According to the *2015 Indicators of Higher Education Equity* report from the Pell Institute and PennAHEAD, the percent of average college costs covered by the maximum Pell Grant has declined from a high of 67 percent in 1975–1976, to a low of 27 percent in 2013. For students from families with annual incomes less than $40,000, the cost of annual college attendance is 74 percent of total family income compared to only 18 percent for students with family incomes of $200,000 (Cahalan et al., 2016). Further, as of 2012, unmet financial need for dependent undergraduates constituted an 84 percent mean net price of total family income to families in the bottom income quartile by 2012 (Mortensen, 2016). Such crippling financial demands on low-income parents severally limit the educational choices and opportunities available for their students.

Educational equity is not just a civil rights issue. It also greatly impacts the financial well-being of the United States in terms of developing a skilled, educated workforce prepared to meet the demands of the new knowledge-based global economy. According to a 2015 National Science Foundation report, 20 percent of all U.S. jobs now require significant knowledge of science, engineering, technology, and math (STEM) and skills related to those disciplines, and that number is growing while the number of workers prepared for STEM careers is shrinking (National Science Foundation Board, 2015). According to a 2015 report from the United States Department of Education, an estimated two-thirds of job openings by 2020 will require postsecondary education or training. Since 2007, nearly all employment growth in the United States has been in jobs requiring some form of postsecondary education, with 8.1 million more jobs for Americans with a bachelor's degree than existed prior to the beginning of the Great Recession in 2007 (Lumina Foundation, 2016). Unfortunately, the United States currently ranks twelfth worldwide in Tertiary-Type A degree attainment for 25–35 year olds (Mortensen, 2016) and could face a major shortage of skilled labor in the future. In a 2016 Business Conditions survey, members of the National Association for Business Economics reported a 31 percent increase in the shortage of skilled labor required by their respective firms and industries.

This national problem is also occurring on a microlevel within Nevada. Although the fast-growing occupations in the state are all projected to require postsecondary training and/or education, Nevada still lags well behind national averages in education spending and degree completion (Nevada Governor's Office of Economic Development, 2017). Only 30 percent of Nevadans age twenty five and older hold a bachelor's degree, ranking the state near the bottom of the United States in postsecondary educational attainment (U.S. Census Bureau, 2010). This lack of education and training has also left Nevada as the state with the highest shortage (32 percent) of current postsecondary education attainment versus job market demands by 2020 (Carnavale, Smith, & Strohl, 2013).

This situation could be difficult to rectify given Nevada's current investment in education. Nevada currently ranks forty-seventh nationally in per-pupil expenditures for K-12 public education, spending $8,026 annually per pupil compared to the $10,763 national average and the $9,200 regional average (2017 Nevada Education Data Book, 2017). Lack of investment per student creates a funding base that negatively impacts the availability of equipment and supplies, functional labs, trained teachers and personnel, and other indispensable resources necessary for successful college and career preparation. Nowhere is this demonstrated more clearly than in the performance of Nevada students on the ACT, a standardized college entrance examination that measures academic knowledge and college readiness (Cline, 2017). In 2016, only 11 percent of Nevada juniors who took the statewide ACT achieved college-ready benchmark scores in the four ACT categories of English, mathematics, reading, and science, compared to the national average of 26 percent of students who met all four (Cline, 2017).

Clearly Nevada has a tremendous need for programs that prepare students for postsecondary education. Given that one in five children in Washoe County, currently live below the poverty line, and 49 percent of students in Washoe County School District are receiving Free and Reduced Lunch (Kemp, 2016), programs, such as Upward Bound, that provide free college preparation services for low-income students are even more critical.

The University's Washoe Grant, the first TRiO grant awarded in the state of Nevada, has been providing college preparatory services to LIFG students since 1967, making it one of the oldest continuously funded classic Upward Bound programs in the nation. The other two Upward Bound programs, the Truckee Grant and the Northwest Grant, were added to the University's slate of TRiO programs in the early 2000s. In the fifty years since Upward Bound began at the University, the three programs have collectively provided services to 4,925 students (E. E. Houston, personal communication, April 17, 2017). At present, the three programs annually serve 186 LIFG students at six target high schools in Washoe and Lyon Counties. To provide rigorous and cutting-edge academic and noncognitive support services that truly prepare students for postsecondary education, the University of Nevada, Reno Upward Bound programs have designed curriculum and activities that develop the critical skills, abilities, and knowledge that participants need for successful high school graduation, postsecondary enrollment, and college graduation.

During the academic year, an Upward Bound (UB) counselor for each grant is embedded in each target school two days per week to provide individualized academic advising and personal counseling. The counselor meets with UB students biweekly, or more, to review courses, grades, assignment completion, attendance, and behavior using real-time data from each school district's database.

The UB counselor provides students advice and assistance in secondary course selection by creating a four-year Academic Plan outlining a rigorous schedule of courses, including dual-enrollment opportunities, for each semester of the student's entire high school career. The counselor also provides mentoring college exploration and admissions information; resources for locating public and private scholarships; assistance completing college admissions and scholarship applications; information on a full range of federal student financial aid programs and benefits; study and test-taking skills; organization and time-management; and leadership development. Further,

UB students work with the counselor to create Education Action Plans, detailing individual student educational, postsecondary, and personal goals each semester.

Academic-year tutoring is offered to students three evenings per week at the University for Washoe and Truckee Upward Bound grant students. College students with excellent grades are hired and trained to serve as tutors for all levels of high school math, English, literature and composition, laboratory science, history, and foreign language. A graduate-level literacy specialist is also available to assist students in improving their reading and writing competencies. Tutoring is conducted one-on-one and in small groups.

For the rural target schools of the Northwest Upward Bound grant, academic year tutoring is offered at the schools three days per week, and through online videoconferencing with student tutors on the University of Nevada, Reno campus. The UB counselor oversees daily operations of all project tutoring components; however, certified Lyon County School District teachers are hired to serve as academic tutors for all levels of high school math, English, literature and composition, laboratory science, history, and foreign language. Project students who need additional writing assistance and high-level STEM courses are also able to access videoconferencing software and laptops with headphones that allow them to connect remotely with college student tutors hired by the program.

An Upward Bound SAT/ACT coordinator provides a mandatory two-hour test-preparation course one night per week at the University for junior and senior UB students during the academic year. The course incorporates the ePrep SAT and ACT online study programs with adaptive diagnostics and personalized feedback to assist students in building the necessary skills to improve standardized test scores. Students receive assistance with registering for the SAT and ACT tests, including fee waivers to take each test at least twice. A similar SAT/ACT preparation course is provided by the UB counselor in the rural target schools.

During the academic year, the project holds monthly College Preparatory Saturday Sessions (CPSS) that bring students to the University for six hours of grade-level programming (GLP) designed to prepare students for success in college. The GLP for freshmen focuses on preparing students for high school academic success and competitive college admissions through developing awareness and skills related to college exploration, service learning, self-awareness, study skills, financial literacy, and leadership. Sophomore GLP focuses on career options and readiness. It includes lessons on résumé building, interview skills, professionalism, one-on-one mock interviews with community members, a Career Day event featuring local professionals in a variety of fields, and college major and career exploration. Junior GLP is built on SAT/ACT preparation and includes test-taking strategies, practice tests, study sessions aimed at each portion of the tests, individualized ePrep online study program modules for skill building, and review of material related to test questions most frequently missed by UB students. The senior GLP covers essential college matriculation topics including college major selection, financial literacy, the completion of college admission applications, FAFSA, and scholarships, information on financial aid programs and benefits, postsecondary course selection, and an overview of college support resources. CPSS also includes a monthly lunchtime student Book Club facilitated by the literacy tutor. Further, the UB Parent Advisory Committee meets during each CPSS session and invites guest speakers to conduct parent workshops on a variety of college readiness topics including economic literacy, financial aid programs, college applications, high school graduation requirements, and LIFG student support in college.

All UB students are offered both educational and cultural activities. To help students complete four hours per semester of required service learning, the Upward Bound programs offer monthly service learning opportunities in collaboration with campus departments such as Social Work and Veteran's Services, as well as community organizations such as the Boys & Girls Club and the American Cancer Society. Students also attend the large Western Association for College Admission Counseling College Fair in Reno each fall. In addition, UB offers students opportunities to attend civic literacy workshops, theater productions, campus lecture series, museum trips, and visits to historical sites. High-performing students are taken on both in-state and out-of-state college tours to help them determine the best possible college fit, and to develop an understanding of the college admissions process.

Each June, all rising seniors are required to attend a two-day, intensive retreat to prepare them for college admissions, the financial aid process, and senior leadership. Workshop topics include college applications, financial aid applications, scholarships, essay writing, and a summer assignment that requires the preparation of a scholarship portfolio including: a résumé, a letter of recommendation request, and a personal statement essay. To best simulate a college-going experience, the Upward Bound programs offer a six-week residential summer academy on the University campus each summer. UB students attend class or lab for six hours a day, five days per week, live in a University residence hall, and eat in the campus dining café.

The Upward Bound programs implement an engaging, project-based thematic curriculum for Summer Academy in which instructors plan interdisciplinary units, incorporating the theme into all courses, and integrating technology so that up to 10 percent of course content is delivered through web-based applications. This type of curriculum promotes critical thinking, culturally responsive teaching, and multimodal learning, and engages students in cooperative learning activities that reinforce concepts and academic skill sets. For example, incorporating the events and evidence from the popular mystery podcast *Serial* across the curriculum provides relevance for students and promotes innovative strategies for incorporating technology to increase STEM skills in the classroom.

The thematic curriculum offers students grade-level appropriate core curriculum courses in math from Algebra 1 through calculus and statistics, English composition and literature, foreign language, and various laboratory sciences to prepare them for a rigorous course of study in the coming year of high school. All students take a college-readiness course designed to foster major and career exploration, improve study skills, and increase standardized tests scores through use of the ePrep online study software for the PSAT, SAT, and/or ACT, depending on grade level. In addition, each student enrolls in an elective class such as art and media production, CrossFit physical conditioning, or drama. Junior and senior students may also take a career internship course as an elective, with seniors able to earn work-study stipends for their internships. The career internship course provides students the opportunity to gain valuable interviewing skills and work experience in assigned campus departments for two hours each day, four days per week. University personnel in those departments serve as mentors and supervisors for the students, and the UB counselor conducts a Friday seminar course that allows students to process their experiences and discuss learning outcomes. All summer academy courses are taught by highly qualified instructors hired from the Washoe County School District (WCSD) or the University, and students who complete summer academy with a 3.25 GPA or higher are awarded one high school credit on their official high school transcript.

During the summer academy, students attend weekly advising with their UB counselor, and daily academic tutoring conducted by trained tutors and resident assistants. To foster a sense of community, support the curriculum, and provide opportunities not usually available to disadvantaged youth, summer academy students are assigned to small resident advisor-led pods. They are offered cocurricular programming each evening, such as weekly community-building exercises, personal vision board creation, the University outdoor summer film festival, a student talent show, and a scavenger hunt applying the principle of triangulation using GPS receivers in the field. Students are also provided cultural and educational field trips, such as visiting the Planetarium, attending various Artown performances in downtown Reno, participating in a spoken word open-microphone night, attending a tour of the Nevada Seismological Lab to witness shake table testing, and manning a hands-on, NASA-based mission to Mars simulation at the Challenger Learning Center of Northern Nevada.

The Upward Bound programs also offer other academic opportunities each summer. Eligible students have the opportunity to apply to a six-week regional Upward Bound Math Science (UBMS) summer program at the University of California, Berkeley, University of California, Santa Cruz, and the University of Hawaii at Mānoa. The project pays transportation fees for students who are selected to attend the STEM-focused UBMS summer programs. In addition, students who have extenuating circumstances that prevent them from attending a residential summer program complete a six-week Online Summer Academy using the ePrep standardized test prep program. Online Summer Academy is supported by a certified teacher hired to check in with students and conduct both walk-in lab and video-conferencing academic tutoring and support. Further, graduating UB seniors immediately matriculating to college in the fall are offered the opportunity to participate in a summer bridge program to aid in their transition to postsecondary education. Upward Bound pays for two college summer school courses for select students, with each UB counselor providing advising, postsecondary course selection advice, and academic support.

The Upward Bound programs also encourage eligible UB students to participate in dual enrollment opportunities, which allow students to simultaneously enroll in credit-bearing college courses while still in high school. However, financial constraints and lack of transportation can be a barrier to dual enrollment for LIFG students, as in most cases, participants must pay for course credit fees and textbooks, as well as find reliable transportation to the postsecondary educational institution. Upward Bound students from the rural, Northwest Grant in Lyon County are able to participate in Western Nevada College's (WNC) Jump Start dual enrollment program. For eligible participants, the host high school covers the cost of enrollment for mathematics, English and other general education college courses, and WNC instructors come to both Fernley and Silver Stage High Schools each day to teach the courses on site (Jump Start College, 2016). Eligible Washoe and Truckee Grant Upward Bound students enrolled in the Washoe County School District (WCSD) can apply to attend Truckee Meadows Community College High School (TMCC), or complete dual enrollment courses through TMCC Jump Start Dual Credit, when scholarship funds are available.

In addition to community college dual enrollment programs, eligible Upward Bound seniors from WCSD have the unique opportunity to participate in the free Pell Experimental Site Initiative (PESI) program at the University of Nevada, Reno. Stemming from the United States Department of Education Dual Enrollment Experiment, PESI is an experimental program in which "participating institutions will be provided a waiver of the specific statutory and regulatory provisions that prevent students who are enrolled in secondary school from receiving Federal Pell Grants for enrollment in Title IV-eligible postsecondary programs" (U.S. Department of Education Federal Student Aid.

Retrieved from https://experimentalsites.ed.gov/exp/approved). In its first year of operation, the PESI program at the University of Nevada, Reno served eight Upward Bound seniors who had a University admissible 3.0 GPA in their core high school classes, completed the FAFSA, and met the income eligibility requirements for a Pell Grant based on halftime enrollment, indicated an interest in majoring in engineering, and placed into college-level pre-calculus based on SAT, ACT, or ACCUPLACER scores.

The Upward Bound programs, Enrollment Services, and the Office of Financial Aid and Scholarships partnered to implement the PESI program. Financial Aid processed the FAFSAs, packaged and awarded the Pell Grants, and handled all reporting to the United States Department of Education. Enrollment Services registered the students in the appropriate courses that worked around their high school schedules, paid for textbooks, and covered parking expenses as necessary. The Upward Bound programs provided group tutoring services tailored for the college math course content the PESI students were encountering. By the end of their senior year, the initial PESI cohort earned a total of ninety-six university credits and a collective 3.4 University GPA. As of summer 2017, ten Upward Bound students have already qualified to participate in PESI for the 2017–2018 academic year.

According to Upward Bound and PESI participant Brianna Meza, "PESI solidified my decision to go on to college. I feel like I am more prepared to tackle the challenges of the future, and have a lowered risk of dropping out. The most beneficial thing about PESI for me was that I got this experience first-hand. I always hear these experiences from college students, and it's good to experience some college first-hand before you get there." (B. Meza Palomar, personal communication, April 10, 2017).

Through intensive college preparatory services such as those described throughout this chapter, the Upward Bound programs at the University of Nevada, Reno continue to exceed the federally outlined objectives for each grant on an annual basis. Table 3.1 details the collective performance results of the Washoe Grant, Truckee Grant, and Northwest Grant for the 2015–2016 academic year (Fittrer, Houston, Valle & Mala, 2017).

FIGURE 3.1. 2015–2016 Annual Performance Report Results, University of Nevada, Reno Upward Bound Programs.

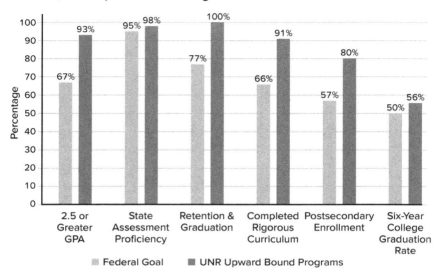

The three classic Upward Bound grants at the University of Nevada, Reno are currently funded through 2021, and will continue to provide innovative and high-quality college preparatory services to LIFG students in Washoe and Lyon Counties. In addition, the University hopes to add two Upward Bound Math Science (UBMS) grants to its precollege offering for the 2017–2021 funding cycle. Given the large population of low-income, first-generation students in Northern Nevada, the fifty-year-old mission of the Upward Bound Programs is still critically relevant today, and the programs remain an important component in helping the University of Nevada, Reno meet its strategic plan and land-grant institution objectives (Johnson & Carman, 2015).

References

Cahalan, M., Perna, L., Yamashita, M., Ross, B., Ruiz, R., Franklin, K. 2015. *Indicators of higher education equity in the United States*, Washington, DC: Pell Institute for the Study of Opportunity in Higher Education, Council for Opportunity in Education (COE) and Alliance for Higher Education and Democracy of the University of Pennsylvania (PennAHEAD).

Cahalan, M., Perna, L., Yamashita, M., Ruiz, R., Franklin, K. 2016. *Indicators of Higher education equity in the United States: 2016 historical trend report*,

Washington, DC: Pell Institute for the Study of Opportunity in Higher Education, Council for Opportunity in Education (COE) and Alliance for Higher Education and Democracy of the University of Pennsylvania (PennAHEAD).

Carnavale, A. P., Smith, N., & Strohl, J. (2013, June). Recovery: Job growth and education requirements through 2020. Retrieved April 11, 2017, from https://cew.georgetown.edu/cew-reports/recovery-job-growth-and-education-requirements-through-2020/

Cline, J. (2017, May 12). *ACT statewide testing performance results: A P-16 CCR opportunity.* Lecture presented at P-16 Council Meeting in Nevada, Reno.

Education Alliance of Washoe County. (2016, June). *Data Profile 2015* (Rep.). Retrieved April 6, 2017, from Education Alliance of Washoe County website: https://ed-alliance.org/wp-content/uploads/2016/06/2015_DataProfile-FINALfinal.pdf

Fittrer, P., Houston, E. E., Valle, D., & Mala, M. M. (2017). *AOSP Highlights 2017* (Rep.). Academic and Opportunity Support Programs.

Galvez, S. & Houston, E. E. (2016, April). *Welcome letter from conference co-chairs.* Western Association of Educational Opportunity Personnel 2016 Annual Conference Program presented in Reno, Nevada.

Johnson, M. A., & Carman, K. R. (2015, January). *Strategic plan 2015–2021: Strategic snapshot* (Rep.). Retrieved May 10, 2017, from University of Nevada, Reno website: https://www.unr.edu/Documents/provost/provosts-office/forms/Strategic%20Plan%20Final%20Jan%202015.pdf.

Jump Start College. (2016). Retrieved April 12, 2017, from http://www.wnc.edu/jump-start/.

Kemp, K. (2017, October). [Washoe County School District Accountability Office Data for 2017 Upward Bound Grant Proposals]. Unpublished raw data.

Lumina Foundation (2016, April). A Stronger Nation: Postsecondary learning builds the talent that helps us rise. Retrieved April 8, 2017, from http://strongernation.luminafoundation.org/report/main-narrative.html

Mortenson, T. (2016, September 1). *Financial barriers to opportunity for higher education.* Lecture presented at Council for Opportunity in Education National Conference in San Diego, California.

National Association for Business Economics. (2016, October). Business Conditions Survey. Retrieved June 23, 2017, from http://nabe.com/nabe/NABE/Surveys/Business_Conditions_Surveys/October_2016_Business_Conditions_Survey_Summary.aspx

National Science Foundation Board. (2015, February 4). Revisiting the STEM workforce—A Companion to science and engineering indicators 2014 (Rep.). Retrieved April 8, 2017, from https://www.nsf.gov/pubs/2015/nsb201510/nsb201510.pdf.

Nevada Governor's Office of Economic Development. (2017). Workforce talent & education. Retrieved May 12, 2017, from http://nv.diversifynevada.com/why/workforce_talent_education/

Nevada Legislative Council Bureau. (2017, April 7). 2017 Nevada education data book (Rep.). Retrieved April 13, 2017, from Nevada Legislative Council Bureau https://www.leg.state.nv.us/Division/Research/Publications/EdDataBook/.

U.S. Census Bureau. (2009, October 21). 2010 Census. Retrieved April 12, 2017, from https://www.census.gov/2010census/.

U.S. Census Bureau Nevada Quick Facts. (2016, July 1). Retrieved May 12, 2017, from https://www.census.gov/quickfacts/table/PST045216/32.

U.S. Department of Education. (2017, October 17). 50th Anniversary Federal TRiO Programs Fact Sheet (Rep.). Retrieved April 4, 2017, from U.S. Department of Education https://www2.ed.gov/about/offices/list/ope/TRiO/TRiO50anniv-factsheet.pdf.

U.S. Department of Education. (2015, July 27). Fact Sheet: Focusing higher education on student success. Retrieved May 12, 2017, from https://www.ed.gov/news/press-releases/fact-sheet-focusing-higher-education-student-success.

U.S. Department of Education federal student aid experiments. (2017, April 4). Retrieved May 17, from https://experimentalsites.ed.gov/exp/approved.

CHAPTER 4

The Wolf Pack First Program for First-Generation Students Wanting to Join the Pack

CAROLINA MARTINEZ, MA

For the last decade, Carolina Martinez has worked as a recruiter in the Office for Prospective Students. She enjoys all types of recruitment, but has a special interest in assisting first-generation and ethnically diverse students. Being a first-generation student herself, Martinez understands the need for the extra assistance to assure students a smooth transition from high school to college. Her passion for this population also motivates her to seek initiatives, such as the Wolf Pack First program that offer personalized assistance to eligible students.

Introduction

Being a first-generation student is not a choice, but being a first-generation student at the University of Nevada, Reno is, and for me it was the best decision ever. As a high school senior in rural Nevada, I was fascinated by how University staff such as Hellen Quan-Lopez in Admissions and Lourdes Gonzales in Financial Aid diligently helped me navigate the system. The VIP treatment did not stop there. Once enrolled at the University I joined the TRiO Scholars program and all my tutors, including Heather Williams, patiently gave me the tools necessary to improve my math and writing skills. Even at my student job, my supervisor, Robert Edgington, became a mentor who continues to guide me in the right direction. Back then I wondered why strangers were so vested in helping me succeed. Now that fifteen years have passed, as a college graduate with a master's degree and an exciting job, I completely understand the desire to help students succeed.

As an admissions counselor myself, I have confirmed that first-generation students' success can only be achieved when everyone is involved. First-generation students must always be offered the extra help needed, should receive answers to the unasked questions, and must find mentors in University staff who will continue reassuring them they can do it. That made a world of a difference for me, and I am glad somebody knew that.

In my ten years working with incoming freshman, I have also learned that the biggest obstacle first-generation students face is the lack of information. Being unaware of how, when, and where to apply for admissions is a barrier. Not understanding the cost of attendance and the opportunities to finance a college education is just as bad. Although parents of first-generation students are eager to help, they deal with frustration when not knowing where to start. It takes a few minutes to sit with them and explain the entire process from beginning to end, and ultimately I get that sigh of relief from them. Unfortunately, it is difficult to reach every first-generation student and give them the quality of assistance needed when time and resources are limited. That is why a few years ago I felt the need to create a program that would provide the same personalized guidance to as many first-generation students as possible. As a result, the Wolf Pack First (WPF) program was created.

The Wolf Pack First Program

The WPF program is a recruitment initiative that originated in the Office for Prospective Students. It seeks to provide essential information as well as personalized assistance to local, high-achieving first-generation students wanting to pursue a college education. A cohort of 200–300 students is selected annually to participate in the program. Students and their parents are invited to the campus throughout the year to attend three conferences where they learn about a variety of college related topics. In addition, students and their parents meet administrative faculty from various departments on campus, which allows them to continue to stay in contact whenever questions arise.

Conference Content

The first WPF conference takes place at the end of the participant's junior year. Students and their parents are introduced to the basics of preparing for college, such as when to apply for admissions, how to apply, important deadlines, financial aid and scholarship opportunities, and academic programs. The second conference takes place in October of their senior year and the focus is to urge students to take action and submit their University of Nevada, Reno admissions and housing applications as well as to submit the Free Application for Federal Student Aid (FAFSA). Students also receive a packet of information about institutional and external scholarship opportunities. The third conference takes place in mid-spring of their senior year. Class schedules, financial aid offers, new-student orientation, and summer school are among the subjects addressed. Institutional support services are also introduced at this time. Although there are only three conferences in the program, students receive constant communication from the Office for Prospective Students throughout the year regarding deadline reminders, campus visit opportunities, upcoming events, and more. Parents are also encouraged to schedule individual appointments with admissions counselors and to participate on a campus tour to get more acclimated to our University.

Process and Reasoning for Student Selection Process

The admissions counselor and school counselors collaborate to select Wolf Pack First participants. The admissions counselor communicates program criteria to the school counselors. Participants must (a) come from a first-generation background, (b) have a strong academic profile, and (c) express an interest to attend college. School counselors then identify eligible candidates and brief them on the benefits of participating in the WPF program. Students next attend an information session led by the WPF program coordinator and are given the opportunity to ask questions and decide whether they want to participate in the program.

The Engine Behind the Program

A strong support system must be established to run the WPF program successfully. It is essential to have support from administrators on a multilevel basis. For instance, a key contributor to the WPF program is Steve Maples, director of undergraduate admissions. He provides guidance and approves calling and texting campaigns and authorizes purchases necessary to run the conferences. He also acts as an advocate when complex logistical barriers arise. Financial aid advisors are also essential collaborators. During the conferences, they conduct presentations on topics such as how financial aid works and the types of aid available. Student volunteers also are a must. They greet and direct families attending the conferences, participate in student panels, and are available for questions at the end of the conferences. Last but not least, it is important to have a formal program committee. Members from the Wolf Pack First Committee run the conferences and come up with creative ways to improve the program year after year. Committee members are likely to come from a first-generation background and hold a genuine interest in helping other first-generation students succeed. They attend monthly meetings, plan and execute the conferences, participate in e-mailing and phone-calling campaigns, and attend and present at the conferences. Seven Wolf Pack First Committee members currently represent various departments on campus, including Admissions, Campus Visits, GEAR UP, Housing, Recruitment, and Student Support Services. Every member strengthens the WPR program by sharing knowledge and expertise from the departments they represent. They are excellent tools not only for giving students the most current information, but also to help the students feel at ease.

A Win-Win Situation for All

Students and Parents

Over the years I have seen first-generation students miss unique institutional opportunities offered to those who meet priority deadlines. For instance, at the University of Nevada, Reno students who participate in early admissions receive priority in getting admitted, on-campus housing, financial aid packages and scholarships, and early class registration. The WPF program works to eliminate that risk for first-generation students by providing a wealth of information early in the process. During the first conference, presentations and distributed literature focus on those important deadlines, items to submit for admission, and detailed instruction on how to do it. That means WPF students and their parents have an equal opportunity to receive priorities that other non-first-generation students do. In addition, since the WPF conferences brings presenters from the different departments, students no longer have to figure out a way to schedule individual departmental appointments on their own. Further, collected conference evaluations have demonstrated that students feel a huge sense of relief when given this information. Parents have also mentioned feeling a sense of empowerment to better help and support their students once they become familiar with all the admissions and financial aid processes.

High School Counselors

Counselors have ever-increasing responsibilities. It is a challenge for them to meet with every first-generation student and his/her parents and explain the college admissions process. Some schools have tried to implement services that just focus on this student population, but, when financial crises arrive, school administrators are forced to eliminate such programs. The WPF program does not intend to replace counselor's or school's guidance, only to complement it. When time and funds are limited, it is strategic for school counselors to partner with colleges and universities who offer programs such as the WPF. Such partnerships become more attractive when they demand minimal efforts from the already busy counselors. For instance, the WPF program only asks that school counselors identify potential candidates and facilitate monthly group meetings between the WPF program coordinator and the participants. In return, counselors receive assistance with guiding their first-generation students as well as updates on their student's application status, for those who have completed proper documentation needed for information-sharing purposes. This type of partnership not only helps students receive the information, but also helps counselors by taking one small task off their plate.

Admission Counselors

Assisting first-generation students on a one-on-one basis is definitely helpful, but assisting 200–300 of them at a time is far more efficient. The WPF program creates the platform to disseminate important information to a larger audience who is likely to share similar struggles, concerns, and fears. Besides being efficient, the WPF program allows admission counselors to meet with the desired population early in the process and give them the information needed for admission and financial aid. Since finances highly influence first-generation students' decision to attend college, helping them qualify for desirable scholarships simplifies the recruitment efforts. In addition, meeting with students early will alert admission counselors about possible concerns that could transform into admission barriers down the road. For instance, students who are not well informed on the admission requirements might take for granted the importance of preparing for and taking the ACT or SAT. If they fail to take them on time, they face the risk of delaying admissions even if they have a strong grade point average. Core credit deficiencies is also of high concern, but when identified early and addressed quickly, the threat of becoming ineligible for admissions is rapidly removed. Taking a proactive recruitment approach offered by the WPF has proven to help admissions counselors eliminate future barriers that could prevent them from recruiting first-generation students.

Student-Retention Services

As a first-generation student, receiving assistance from many individuals on campus, including the coordinators in the TRiO Scholars Program and the University's student cultural center, "The Center, Every Student. Every Story.," greatly contributed to my college success. Whenever I was stressed about finances or failing academically, somebody was there to provide solutions. That made a difference between helping me become a college graduate or a dropout. Knowing the effectiveness of these programs becomes essential to incorporating them into the WPF program. During the last conference, coordinators from departments such as the First in the Pack and the TRiO Scholars program are given the time to present and recruit students to their programs. Strategically, this works because the assistance from the WPF program is only available to students until the end of their senior year. Coordinators from other student retention services, such as the the Center and the Office of Financial Aid, are also able to present and recruit students to use their services.

Parent and Student Testimonial

It is important to collect information on every event to measure the effectiveness or lack of it. For the WPF program, we measure success through casual conversations with participants during conferences and a short survey collected at the end of each conference. According to data collected from surveys, students in the WPF program and their parents mostly value information received on admissions, steps to apply for admissions, cost of attendance, important deadlines, financial aid and scholarships, as well as student support services offered to current University of Nevada, Reno students. The biggest complaint received from one of the conferences was regarding the distance the respondent had to walk from the parking lot to the program venue. Positive and negative feedback is considered when preparing for the next program. Parent testimonials are carefully analyzed because the parents are the ones supporting their student's decision to attend college, and it is important that they, too, have a positive experience.

Ricardo Lucio Sr., the father of a former WPF program participant from the class of 2016, frequently approached me to thank me for having allowed his son to participate in the WPF program. He said that he and his wife had always tried to take an active role in their son's academics from an early age, but when it came to college admissions, the cost of attendance, and financial aid, they had no idea where to begin. Those conversations made me feel so happy to be a coordinator for the WPF program. Although it takes a lot of time and energy to run, it is all well worth it. Currently, Ricardo Lucio is enrolled at the University of Nevada, Reno studying business management. He joined a community-service-based fraternity on campus and volunteers for the WPF program every time he has the opportunity. He tells me he enjoys giving back to the program that has opened so many possibilities for him.

Program's Future Vision

Three years ago, when the first WPF program cohort was selected, the vision for the program was to simply help first-generation students attend college by providing them with the information needed in a timely fashion. Over the years that vision has persisted, but new goals have been added. First, the Wolf Pack First Committee intends to keep growing the program and serve more first-generation students per school. Second, we hope to increase partnerships and include more on- and off-campus organizations that can strengthen the WPF program. Third, we desire to have funding for the program allocated earlier in the academic year to better plan for the conferences. We do not claim to be experts on event planning or all issues related to first-generation students, but we do claim to share a strong interest: to help first-generation students succeed.

PART II

Resources for First-Generation, Income-Qualified Students

An old mantra states *it takes a village to raise a child*; the equivalent is true on a campus community whose goal is to help every student succeed. A growing collection of student services provides academic and personal resources to support student success. Since the 1960s, the University of Nevada, Reno has made a concerted effort to enhance the resources that it offers to low-income, first-generation students—services that enrich the educational experience. The following section highlights resources, some celebrating more than fifty years, and others in their second year, available at the University of Nevada, Reno to help students thrive.

CHAPTER 5

Developing Pipeline Programs for Scholar Students of Color

QUENTIN OWENS, MA

Quentin Owens is the manager for Scholar Recruitment and Admissions at the University of Nevada, Reno. In his role, he works to recruit students who are academically gifted. Owens earned a master's of education in secondary education from the University of Nevada, Reno.

Introduction

As the University of Nevada, Reno's incoming freshman class continues to grow, there is a greater need to make sure that this growth reflects the population of Nevada. Nevada is one of the most ethnically diverse Mountain West states in the country. The University celebrates diversity and the outcomes of having an ethnically diverse student body. This diverse incoming class did not happen by chance. Strategic measures formed a steady pipeline of diverse scholar students enrolling into the University of Nevada, Reno. These measures were developed out of the goodwill of the Student Services Division, which secured funding, promoted scholarly opportunities, and directed entry into graduate programs.

Pipeline Programs

In 2008, representatives of the Student Services Division met with Dr. Larry Smith, a higher education consultant whose expertise includes recruitment. Dr. Smith suggested that our institution must have a stronger presence in the state of Nevada. He suggested offering early, meaningful outreach programs that would be beneficial for the overall good of the state and the University. So, we expanded the Early College and Dual Credit programs.

Early College and Dual Credit are programs that allow high school students to take college-level courses. These courses can be physically taught at high schools, at college campuses, or through distance education. After the completion of these courses, students receive high school credit and college credit. We made an effort to increase ethnically diverse students of color into our Early College and Dual Credit Programs by:

- Promoting Early College and Dual Credit at lower socioeconomic high schools and charter schools.
- Attending community events geared toward ethnically diverse peoples.
- offering Spanish language informational sessions.
- collaborating with local school districts equity and diversity departments.

We developed rigorous, but attainable admission requirements. This allowed us to identify students who would be successful at the college level. We did not lower the University standards for admissions into the program, nor offer an alternative admissions for the program. The student participants in the program were directed into three curriculums. Curriculum 1 focused on introductory science labs. University faculty members taught these labs. Curriculum 2 focused on students who said they wanted to complete their "core" University courses. The core University courses satisfied University freshman/sophomore core and high school graduation requirements. Curriculum 3 focused on students who had completed Advanced Placement Curriculum at their designated high school but wanted to take courses to help them get into advanced college curriculums/research labs.

Within these three curriculums, we were able to customize our communication flow and one-on-one contact so we could develop a "pipeline" of scholar students of color.

The University designated a special recruitment representative to act as a liaison between the school districts, the Provost's Office (different academic schools/colleges/Honors Program), and the Student Services Division (Financial Aid, Tutoring, Admissions) for these students. Many of these students would qualify for admissions into highly competitive institutions, so it was necessary to have at least one designated faculty position to focus on relationship-building with these students and their families.

The designated faculty member would meet directly with parents and guardians throughout the whole process, which included orientations, FAFSA Nights, college recruitment programs, and specially designed tours. Depending on the level of research that the student was involved in at the University, they were encouraged to continue that research as an incoming freshman. The special recruitment representative would lobby academic departments for scholarship and lab funds to secure funding for these scholar-students if they decided to attend the University full-time their freshman year. During this same time, we became a full member of the National Merit Scholarship Corporation. Because we are a National Merit Sponsoring Institution, we were able to sponsor students of color who qualified as National Merit Finalists. We also began to recognize the achievements of students who were designated National Merit Semifinalists, National Achievement Finalists, and National Hispanic Recognition Scholars with institution funding and academic scholarships.

Because of our early outreach secondary programs, Early College/ Dual Credit: core dual credit classes, AP labs, and scholar credit labs, we were able to make the better "recruitment" pitch to these scholar students of color to stay in-state and receive an amazing academic opportunity that could propel them to one of the top graduate programs in the United States. Some of these students participated in national and international fellowship opportunities and won them.

We became the institution of choice in the state of Nevada for Scholar students of color due to our early outreach efforts that questioned and answered what type of students could best benefit from a Nevada education. Now we have a successful pipeline for students of color, and have amazing alumni who are enrolled in graduate schools, and who have ranked their undergraduate education equal or superior to their peers who studied at top undergraduate institutions.

CHAPTER 6

Recruiting and Retaining Transfer Students

KARI EMM, MA, SELENE RANGEL, MA,
and DAWN AESCHLIMANN, MA

Kari Emm is a current doctoral student at the University of Nevada, Reno in the Equity and Diversity program with an emphasis in higher education. She has spent nine years as the transfer recruitment coordinator for the University where she has gained her expert knowledge in transfer practices and programs. Her research interests include American Indian students and barriers associated with attending postsecondary institutions.

Selene Rangel is a graduate of the University of Nevada, Reno where she earned a bachelor's in criminal justice and a master's degree in educational leadership. Rangel has been dedicated to recruiting and retaining historically underrepresented minorities and serves as an academic advisor in the Division of Health Sciences.

Dawn Aeschlimann has been working at the University of Nevada, Reno since 2007, primarily at the University Advising Center. She teaches an Academic and Career Exploration course and has a passion for working with students. Aeschlimann's focus is on prospective and undecided transfer students, assisting in their major exploration and academic success.

The United States is becoming a more diverse country every year. This in turn creates a unique situation for all educational systems and the support they provide for students. Community colleges in recent years have seen an upward trend of diverse students entering their institutions. In this chapter, transfer students and their trends will be the focus. The chapter will first identify what transfer students look like today and how this profile is comparable to the students of Nevada. It will then give statistical demographical data regarding the University of Nevada, Reno by using transfer student data provided by the University. Lastly, it will discuss the importance of transfer student advising, programming, and how these services can contribute to less transfer shock and more future initiatives for the University of Nevada, Reno.

Comparison of Transfer Students in the State of Nevada

Transfer Student Data by Ethnicity

Typically, there is little differentiation in the characteristics used to describe new freshmen, regardless of whether they are attending a community college or a four-year institution. However, this is a misleading simplification as community college students are very different from traditional freshmen at a four-year institution. A descriptive comparison study by the United States Department of Education, National Center for Education Statistics (2003–2004) found that "community college students were more likely to be: African American or Hispanic; financially independent; first-generation college students; less academically prepared; working part- or full-time during college; having lower degree aspirations; attending college part-time; delaying enrollment into college following high school; receiving less financial aid; and earning a lower GPA during the first year of college" (Seidman, 2012, p. 144). An additional study by the National Center for Education Statistics (NCES) and reported that "of the students who entered a community college with the intent of transferring to a four-year institution and graduating with a bachelor's degree, only about 20–25 percent ever achieved this goal" (Harlow & Bowman, p. 513). Community college students require more attention, not because they are incapable of success but because of the continuous barriers they have to overcome. Also, because of their diverse upbringing, transitioning into campus, whether it be at a four-year or community college, can be challenging.

The changing demographics of the nation is also being seen in the state of Nevada. According to the Nevada Department of Education and Enrollment for 2016–2017, there are 467,105 students from pre-K to twelfth grade in the public school system. The ethnicity breakdown for these grade levels are: Hispanic, 199,350; white, 157,242; black, 51,239; multiracial, 28,870; Asian, 26,049; and American Indian/Alaskan Native, 4,355; with Washoe County School District enrolling 66,671 students. Enrollment data shows that Hispanic/Latino students are taking the lead, and research shows they will most likely start at a community college. However, with this ethnic group also comes the aforementioned community college profile of being first-generation, low-income, working full time, etc. (Nevada Department of Education, 2016).

The state's demographics affect the University of Nevada, Reno. Transfer students at the University make up a third of new incoming students every year. The Office of Student Persistence Research at UNR reported that in 2016 transfer students were between the ages of 20–22 and had an average GPA of a 3.20. The ethnicity of the transfer students was 61 percent white; 22 percent Hispanic; 4 percent Asian or Pacific Islander; 4 percent multiethnic; 2 percent black; 1 percent Native American; 5 percent unknown; and 2 percent nonresident. It also showed that many transfer students are predominantly pursuing liberal arts degrees (Transfer profile, p.6). The transfer student population attending the UNR mirrors the state's demographics with the Hispanic student population growing exponentially. However, the Hispanic student population does not reflect the overall trend of retention rates. The six-year graduation rate by ethnicity for the 2010 cohort was American Indian/Alaskan Native, 47.2 percent; Pacific Islander, 9.1 percent; Asian, 67.5 percent; black, 45.2 percent; Hispanic/Latino, 49 percent; white, 54.5 percent; nonresident, 57.1 percent; and multiethnic, 52.2 percent, with a total six-year graduation rate of 54.3 percent (The Center, 2016)

Transfer Student Programming

Silver State Transfer Program

UNR's transfer student staff created programs specifically to eliminate some of the barriers that many transfer students encounter. The first program, the Silver State Transfer Program (SSTP), is a co-admissions program between the University of Nevada, Reno and Nevada community colleges. The program allows students attending Nevada community colleges to have dual-enrollment at the University. Students in the program get access to University services and have the opportunity to work with an advising specialist from both the community college and the University of Nevada, Reno. The goal of the program is to assist students in their educational endeavors from their community college to the University and create a seamless transition to the University upon completion of their associate's degree. Once accepted into the program, students develop an academic plan with a University academic advisor who works with them throughout their time in the program. Working with an advisor gives students certainty about degree-applicable classes and how they will transfer to the University.

To be admitted into the SSTP, students must have completed at least one college-level English and math course, must maintain a minimum 2.0 grade point average, and must submit an unofficial transcript with their application. Students in the program are in a variety of majors. However, the program is most beneficial for students majoring in engineering, education, and journalism. There are currently thirty-two students in the SSTP, with a majority attending Truckee Meadows Community College (TMCC). Eight co-admission students will be completing their associate's degree this semester and will fully transfer to the University in the Fall semester.

The program focuses on TMCC and Western Nevada College (WNC). There are plans to expand the program to the rest of the community colleges in the state, increase the number of students, and provide more incentives for students to participate. A summer component of the SSTP is also being developed to recruit students at community colleges in rural and Southern Nevada.

Transfer Admissions Program (TAP)

Another program created by UNR is the Transfer Admissions Program (TAP), which is designed to give students an opportunity to continue their education and ultimately obtain a bachelor's degree. The program allows students to prepare early and ensure they are ready to transfer to the University. TAP workshops are held once a month at Truckee Meadows Community College and Western Nevada College. Holding the workshops at the community college campus makes it easier for prospective transfer students to meet with UNR representatives and get their questions answered.

The workshop consists of an admissions and academic advising presentation that covers admission requirements, the application process, transfer agreements, and transfer academic advising. Students can also schedule individual appointments to work with an admissions representative or an academic advisor. Many students use the time to submit their applications and clarify major requirements. Students who attend the TAP workshop are usually those who are ready to transfer. Others attend earlier to ensure they are on the right path to transfer.

The second component to the TAP is an email list that provides an excellent way for students to stay informed about important deadlines, scholarships, job postings, and events. Students are added to the list after the workshops and can be removed from the list at any time. As of fall 2016 there were 416 from TMCC and 212 from WNC on this electronic mailing list. TAP is currently only at TMCC and WNC; however, there are plans to extend the program to community colleges in Southern Nevada.

Why Advising Is Essential for Transfer Students

Transfer Student Advising

Transfer students are coming in with some college experience, but there are many factors that can cause what Hills (1965) refers to as "transfer shock." This can result in a lower GPA in the transfer student's first term at the new institution and may lead to some transfer students' early departure from the new institution. The concern is that these students confront many multidimensional issues that often go unnoticed. It is important for institutions to continue their research and growth in transfer resources such as academic advising.

Each institution has different policies and procedures, and a large part of advising is connecting students with resources and explaining relevant policies. It is the student's responsibility to understand their transfer report at their new institution and, within their advising appointment, they have the opportunity to review and ask questions regarding their transfer courses. Academic advisors play a key role in easing transfer student transitions to decrease transfer shock.

All incoming transfer students to UNR have mandatory academic advising at the University of Nevada, Reno to assist with academic success, retention, and graduation rates. Academic advising is essential for transfer students, to get them on the right track and to make sure that they are in the correct major to achieve their academic goals. Students will gain knowledge about University requirements, core requirements, major requirements, and academic resources. They have the opportunity to set up a graduation plan using the planner in MyNEVADA to assist them to stay on track to graduate in a timely manner.

Future Initiatives for Transfer Students

Transfer Center

The changing demographics of the typical community college student are accompanied by the barriers of socialization and transition into a four-year institution. "Socialization occurs through networks, such as peers and family" (Reason & Renn, p. 65). This is where community colleges and universities must work together and build a strong support system, especially for underrepresented students who might already have barriers unrelated to college such as financial stresses and lack of family support. They can do this by initiating stronger transfer-friendly environments. Currently, transfer centers do not exist at any of the institutions for transfer students, making it more difficult to integrate, receive adequate advising, and feel supported. Most of the responsibility has trickled down to advising centers, which tend to be overwhelmed with day-to-day student advising and have little time for transfer-specific questions. Transfer students tend to get confused, lost, and misled when transitioning from one institution to another. This often happens when they ask and receive incorrect information because they approach the wrong department. If there were transfer centers, students would not have to look for answers, but would have a place and person to assist them. The transfer centers would also assist in the transition and socialization for transfer students, making them feel more welcomed and prepared. With the growing Hispanic/Latino student population, and that being the largest ethnic demographic for transfer students, a transfer center could be essential to their success. The transfer center could also assist in making the University of Nevada, Reno a successful Hispanic Serving Institution.

Other Future Initiatives

The transfer staff is always looking for innovative ways to recruit and retain students at the University of Nevada, Reno. Below are some future initiatives for transfer students depending on resources and staff dedicated to their achievements:

- Marketing materials translated to Spanish
- A Spanish website for transfer students
- A nontraditional transfer student resource guide and website
- Summer programming for high-achieving, underrepresented, transfer students in STEM.
- A successful transfer student mentorship program
- Assessments to gauge transfer student success and completion

Conclusion

The community college student reflects the changing landscape of America. "In general, the community colleges will sustain their enrollments because the demand for postsecondary education will remain high. By 2020 they will enroll eight million students, or nearly 43 percent of all higher education" (Cohen, Brawer, & Kisker, p. 441). In Nevada, community colleges will sustain but will only be successful if they provide the right services to the changing demographics of transfer students. This is also true for the four-year universities. Today's students are facing more challenges than ever before because they are more diverse than ever, and have more responsibilities. This is where the community colleges and universities need to work closer to provide support. The University of Nevada, Reno does have some programming, and it is showing success. However, more resources and staff need to be dedicated to the transfer student initiative for it to be truly successful.

References

Cohen, A. M., Brawer, F. B., & Kisker, C. B. (2014). *The American community college.* San Francisco. 6th Edition.

Harlow, Alicia J., and Sharon L. Bowman. *Examining the career decision self-efficacy and career maturity of community college and first-generation students. Journal of Career Development* 43.6 (2016): 512–25. *ERIC.* Web. 14 Mar. 2017.

Hills, John R. *Transfer shock--the academic performance of the junior college transfer.* N.p.: n.p., 1965. *ERIC.* Web. April 28, 2017.

Nevada Department of Education (2016). 2016–2017 School Year Student Counts for Nevada.

Public Schools. Retrieved from: http://www.doe.nv.gov/DataCenter/Enrollment/.

Office of Student Persistence Research-University of Nevada Reno (2016). "Transfer Student Profile Comparison from 2014 to 2016."

Renn, K. A. R. R. D. (2012). *College Students in the United States*. Somerset: John
    Wiley & Sons, Incorporated.

Seidman, A. L. S. M. A. (2012). *College Student Retention*. Blue Ridge Summit, PA:
    Rowman & Littlefield Publishers.

The Center, Every Student, Every Story. (2016). Annual Report 2016. Retrieved from:
    http://www.unr.edu/Documents/student-services/cultural-diversity/annual-
    reports/CSCD%20Annual%20Report%202016.pdf.

Tinto, V. (2012). *Completing College*. Chicago: University of Chicago Press.

CHAPTER 7

Financial Aid as College Access and Degree Completion

LOURDES GONZALES

Lourdes Gonzales is the associate director of the Student Financial Aid and Scholarships Office of the University of Nevada, Reno. Gonzales earned a bachelor of science degree in business administration with emphasis in information systems and a master of science degree in counseling and educational psychology with emphasis in educational technology. She is an active member of associations of financial aid administrators: Nevada Association of Financial Aid Administrators, Wisconsin Association of Student Financial Aid Administrators, and National Association of Student Financial Aid Administrators.

"Financial support is one of the biggest contributors to my success. Having the ability to know that my classes are paid for allows me to focus entirely on my education without the distraction of financial burden. I know many people who struggle with paying for classes and it negatively effects not only their time that they can dedicate to schoolwork, but also having the thought of upcoming payments can be distracting. I have been lucky to have financial aid up to this point and I feel that with continued support, I will continue to have success in school."

—Fourth-Year Student

"I come from a low-income family. My dad is retired, he does not make enough money to be able to send me to college. It is a daily struggle seeing my parents deal with medical bills and medications they need to pay for. My family is immensely tight with money, paying for me to attend a university has been a stressful topic. My dream has always been to attend the University of Nevada, Reno; however, if my parents cannot afford it, I will not have the opportunity to learn there. I am the only one out of three siblings to go to college because my parents could not afford to pay for my brothers' education."

—Prospective Student

We hear stories like these in our daily interactions with students and parents. The Financial Aid Office mission is to provide our diverse student population with access to postsecondary education by rewarding individual achievements and by reducing the financial barriers that would otherwise prevent or inhibit qualified students from attending the University of Nevada, Reno. The Higher Education Act (HEA) was passed in 1965 with a clearly articulated goal: to provide access to higher education for students who otherwise would be unable to attend. We take that message very seriously. The following will describe how the Financial Aid Office supports students and the institutional goal of their timely degree completion.

Financial Aid Overview

Many categories of financial aid are available to our students, including grants, loans, work-study, and scholarships. The federal government is the main source of funds, followed by institutional, state, and private-sector sources. The total number of financial aid recipients and the total amount awarded increase every year. Comparing award year 2011–2012 to award year 2016–2017, the total number of recipients and the total amount given to students increased by 30 percent and 40 percent respectively.

- More than 70 percent of our students complete the Free Application for Federal Student Aid (FAFSA).
- 90 percent of new freshmen and more than 70 percent of the total student population receive some kind of aid.
- Almost 30 percent receive the Federal Pell Grant.
- More than 40 percent of our undergraduate and 30 percent of our graduate students take out loans to finance their education.
- About 35 percent of our freshmen receive institutional scholarships.
- More than 45 percent of our undergraduate students receive need-based aid.

- More than 60 percent of our new freshmen and almost 40 percent of our total undergraduate student population receive the Governor Guinn Millennium Scholarship.
- More than 200 students complete our financial aid application for non-FAFSA eligible students. Applicants include international and DACA students.

Parents and students often come across the terms need-based aid and merit-based aid during their preparation for college. Let's explore these two types of financial aid.

Need-Based Aid

Grants, subsidized loans, and work-study are three types of aid that students are awarded based upon a calculation of financial need. We use the federal government's methodology to figure out a student's Expected Family Contribution (EFC). The calculation utilizes the data from the Free Application for Federal Student Aid (FAFSA). Since funds from institutional and state sources are limited, aid from these sources goes to the neediest students who complete their applications by the priority deadline. A need-based *grant* is a gift that you need not pay back. *Work-study* opens up jobs to students on campus. The government pays for the interest on *subsidized loans* while the student is in college or while the loan is in deferment.

> "Finances have never been an easy thing for my family. I grew up in a family of five, and my father was the only one with a job. As an undocumented student, it was a constant struggle to help the family pay for day-to-day items as I could not get a job without having applied for the Deferred Action for Childhood Arrivals, which was also expensive. But once I did receive my work permit, I began working late nights. Aside from being from a low-income family, I do not get the opportunity to apply for federal financial student aid. DACA allows me to work in the United States, but I do not get to apply for the Pell Grant, which would have saved my family $5,000 of work. Financial aid would help me attain my educational goals that could not be

reached without the help of my family and their long hours at work. I know funds are limited and money is tight, but even the smallest contributions have the greatest impacts on my future."

—First-Year Student

Since only citizens or eligible noncitizens can file a FAFSA, we offer an application for financial aid for non-FAFSA-eligible students, such as international, DACA, and undocumented students, who are not eligible for Pell Grants or federal student loans. However, there are funds from institutional, state, and private sources that are available to them. We used Institutional Methodology to determine eligibility for scholarships, grants, and institutional work-study that require demonstrated need.

Merit-Based Aid

Merit-based aid generally comes as scholarships. Similar to grants, scholarships do not need to be repaid and are sourced by the state of Nevada, institutional funds, or private agencies. Scholarships at the University of Nevada, Reno are generally awarded on student merit; they may reward outstanding students for academic performance, creativity, career field choices, athletic ability, or other reasons.

Pack Advantage—A Promise to Our Neediest Nevada Students

The Pack Advantage program has been established to ensure access to a university education to in-state students from low-income families. vice president for student services, Shannon Ellis, explains that "the University has made the commitment that any Nevada resident, Pell student admitted and enrolled full time, who files a FAFSA on time will have tuition, fees and books covered by our University for four years— as long as they remain Pell-eligible and in good academic standing." Because the Pell Grant eligibility requires high levels of need, it is used as an indicator of low-income. We understand that financial pressure can mean the difference between enrolling in college or not, persisting in classes or not, completing a degree or not. Because two-thirds of new jobs in the next decade are expected to require a postsecondary credential (Carnavale, 2013), UNR's promise to needy students can have untold impact on their future lives.

Since its inception in 2010, Pack Advantage has benefited thousands of students each year, making it possible for students to attend college by eliminating or significantly reducing their cost of attendance and allowing students to concentrate on their studies rather than having to work more hours. Pack Advantage helps students like the one below.

> My plan of attending the University of Nevada, Reno began in the ninth grade. After hours of research, it did not take long to realize that higher education would cost far more than my family could ever offer. Financial aid of any amount would benefit my family of five, as my parents aim to send both my sibling and me to college this year. My parents never had the opportunity to save up for my education during their struggle with constant lay-offs. My father is currently unemployed and my mother's income as a sales manager supports our family week to week. Since the day I turned the legal age to hold a job, I have been working Monday through Friday to help maintain my household's daily necessities. My determination to become the first member of my family to go to college and my desire to help the community in the field of health care, has given me the persistent drive to succeed in every aspect of high school.
>
> —Prospective Student

Financial Aid as a Completion Pathway

Institutional leaders across the country are focused on building completion pathways to ensure that more students succeed in postsecondary education and make smooth transitions to careers (Reichert, 2012). According to NASFAA, the goal of Title IV student aid historically has been to ensure access to higher education, but in recent years, the high cost of college and the call for fiscal austerity at the federal level have led to increasing emphasis on college completion as a policy goal—that is, student success. As students face an increasing student loan debt burden, graduation and completion rates are taking on a more significant role in policy discussions.

It takes about 120 credits to complete a degree at the University of Nevada, Reno. Because those who enroll in only twelve credits per term, the minimum to be considered full-time, will take at least an additional two semesters to complete a degree and incur additional student loan debt, the Nevada System of Higher Education has embarked on a campaign to increase per-year credit enrollment.

30-to-Complete Campaign

To encourage students to take thirty credits each academic year (the *30-to-Complete* campaign), the Office of Financial Aid and Scholarships provides grants and scholarships to students who enroll in thirty credits a year and who meet need- or merit-based eligibility.

- When students complete more credits each semester, they can be on track to graduate in four years. It is simple math: twelve credits per term=five years for a typical bachelor's degree; fifteen credits per term=four years for a typical bachelor's degree.
- The less time a student is in school, the less debt students accrue from tuition, fees, books, food, housing, and other expenses. The average loan debt for any extra year is $8,000 and this is without including parents' loans.
- The sooner a student finishes her degree, the sooner she can start into her career. In Nevada, a person with a bachelor's degree earns $18,000 more per year than a person with only a high school diploma.

How do we support Nevada's 30-to-Complete campaign?

- Institutional scholarship and grants for students with a plan of study of thirty credits a year
- Millennium Scholarship—incentive for taking more than twelve credits
- Year-Round Pell

Financial aid would impact my education in a very important way. My mom just lost her job and will not be able to help pay for my tuition. Receiving financial aid would let me work less because I am going to have to work a job or multiple jobs. To help relieve the financial burden of my tuition there are some options that I have, but they have pluses and minuses to them. First, I could take less credits a semester and spread out my education across more years, enabling me to pay for tuition and receive good grades to graduate. Second, I could take out student loans but with the tradeoff that I would in the end pay more money because of interest. This wouldn't solve my financial crisis but put me in debt. The impact of financial aid could be immense. I could work one job while receiving financial aid to pay for school. With support and if I work hard, I could graduate in four years with a good degree, great experience, and have a promising future.

—Second Year Student

Millennium Scholarship

In 1999, Governor Kenny Guinn's Millennium Scholarship initiative was enacted into law. This offers Nevada high school graduates (with a GPA of 3.25) free or reduced tuition to in-state universities and colleges. Our state has seen a significant, positive impact—more than double the number of students are attending Nevada colleges and universities—since the program began. In order to support the 30-to-Complete initiative, the 2015 Legislature passed Senate Bill 128. Millennium students receive funding for up to 15 credits per semester. After the implementation of this new measure, we have seen a significant number of students respond to the incentives by taking more credits per semester. They definitely benefit from a timelier degree completion.

Pell Year Round

Financial aid is what allows me to have an education. I have taken student loans out, but I am still paying the difference out of pocket every semester. I work 32 hours a week to pay for bills and school, and am often finding myself either working, in class, or doing homework all day, every day. I also take two classes every summer in an effort to graduate from my engineering program in four years, but neither class is covered by scholarships or loans, and are entirely out of my pocket. I would like to drop some hours at work to increase my focus in class, and achieve better grades, but I am unable to without grants or scholarships.

—Fourth-Year Student

The federal Pell Grant is a form of need-based federal student aid available to low-income students. Pell Grants have traditionally been used to pay for a student's fall and spring terms, but demand for a year-round option has increased in recent years. Students such as this senior received good news in the 2017 budget agreement: Starting summer 2018, our students became able to receive additional Pell Grant funding if they enroll in at least six credits during the summer. This provision should help thousands of low-income students at our institution to graduate in four years and with less debt.

Expanding Need-Based Gift Aid to Low-Middle Income Students

> I come from an average, middle-income family; this means that for the past two years the only financial aid that I have qualified for is loans. It would not be as difficult to pay for school if my parents could afford to help. As it is, I am completely dependent on loans and the Millennium Scholarship. I am already facing thousands of dollars in debt that has collected over a two year period.
> —Third-Year Student

Need-based aid has a major effect on keeping students from dropping out (Alon, 2011). For every extra $100 in need-based aid, low- and middle-income students have an increased chance of persisting. Alon found that this has the greatest effect among the lower middle-income quartile, the group that historically has had the lowest persistence and completion rates to begin with. On the other hand, he finds that for upper middle-income students there is little relationship between receiving aid and dropping out and that for high-income students, need-based aid did not influence whether or not they dropped out. Clearly these results suggest that if an institution is seeking to get the most efficient use of financial aid funds, aid should be concentrated on lower-middle and low-income students.

Low-income students are well-served at our institution. An indicator of low-income status is the eligibility for the Pell Grant. These students, in addition to receiving the Pell Grant, often receive additional need-based gift aid from institutional and state sources such as the Pack Advantage. Nevertheless, low middle-income students, those whose familial income sits right above the Pell cutoff, often find loans to be their only source of funding, although we make every effort to allocate funds to this section of students. Money is critical to their success, and our administration is working on expanding their gift-aid and work-study opportunities.

Access and opportunity are two precious words. Financial assistance makes it possible for many students to attend college. But our commitment to our students does not end with their arrival; we want our students to succeed, to enjoy their college experience, and to graduate in a timely manner as the start to a rewarding future.

References

Alon, S. (2011). Who benefits most from financial aid? The heterogeneous effect of need-based grants on students' college persistence. *Social Science Quarterly*, 92(3), 807–829.

Carnevale, A. P., Rose, S. J., & Cheah, B. (2013). *The college payoff: Education, occupations, lifetime earnings.* Georgetown.

Reichert, Katrina (June 2012). Policy Bulletin. *Aid and Innovation How Federal Financial aid Policy Impacts Student Success and How States Can Respond,* 2.

Reimagining financial aid to improve student access and outcomes, NASFAA, 6.

CHAPTER 8

Nevada Money Mentors

Integration of Financial Literacy into Financial Aid

AMY NELSON

> Amy Nelson is a financial specialist at the University of Nevada, Reno and manages the financial literacy program, Nevada Money Mentors. In her role, Nelson strives to empower students with financial knowledge and resources so that they make informed, confident decisions about their money.

I will never forget meeting one University of Nevada, Reno student.

She walked into the office effervescent with energy. She had an extreme eagerness to learn, with a dream of becoming the next best teacher in this great nation. She was the first in her family to attend college, and she carried pride in what her future held. Not only did she plan on making a difference to thousands of students in her lifetime, but she would study abroad, purchase her own means of transportation so she wouldn't have to walk to work anymore, pay off her student loans as quickly as possible, someday pay for her own wedding, buy a home, have children, travel more, and all the while ensure she still had money to send back home to her family on a regular basis. These are the dreams of one Nevada student—a hardworking, first-generation, full-time student.

But, financially she was struggling. She was losing the battle of money management, coming up short on a monthly basis, not understanding how she was falling behind. Living in the moment of experiences was taking a toll on her bank account. She needed help. And, she was not alone.

- 72 percent of Americans feel out of control when it comes to money (American Psychological Association, 2015).
- 61 percent of Americans live paycheck to paycheck (Shin, 2014).
- The number-one reason for leaving college is money (Gates Foundation, 2016).
- 92 percent of students use credit cards to pay for educational expenses (Credit Donkey, 2014).
- Combined student loan debt is more than $1.5 trillion (McGurran, 2018).
- About four in ten of those ages 18–24 currently have student loan debt (Cilluffo, 2017).
- 45 percent of Nevadans live in liquid asset poverty (Prosperity Now, 2017).

"College is an ideal time to gain personal and economic independence. Aside from striving to graduate debt-free, students should take the initiative to master their finances" (An, 2014). Well-informed students are far more likely to become economically sound, civic leaders, and productive members of our communities. But we don't talk about personal finances enough, and we are not formally educated on a topic that affects us every day . . . until now. . . .

We agree that when we teach our students about money, we teach them about life (Berkowitz, 2014), and that's why we created the Nevada Money Mentors (NMM) Financial Literacy Outreach Program at the University of Nevada, Reno.

A major focus of NMM is our financial coaching program, where we regularly meet with students in one-on-one appointments. Participants of financial coaching make their own personalized budgets, gain a better understanding of credit, and understand how to manage student loans and scholarships effectively to graduate on time.

In precoaching appointments, students assess their confidence in personal money management by completing a Financial Capability Scale, FCS (Collins, 2013). On an eight-point scale most students' average four at their first coaching session and after completion of coaching, which usually takes about four to six visits, the students' FCS jumps to a seven.

Coaching is strengths-based, and over time student habits and behaviors shift in a positive direction because it helps students take responsibility for their own financial security. Here's what some of our students say about financial coaching:

It's really nice to be able to sit down and look at the overall picture. It's amazing that our money is where a lot of unrest lies and to be able to walk away with a plan is good, it's really good.

—UNR Alumni

I learned how to budget and how to "pay myself" every month as opposed to paying off debts such as credit cards. Coaching was very eye-opening because I was used to estimating or giving an approximation on where my money goes but it's a different task to play with the actual numbers. I also built better habits as time went on. I definitely noticed a shift in my thinking.

—UNR Graduate Student

In my coaching sessions I feel like I take away more understanding of my financial situation and how to work toward goals and plan. I was able through a plan created by coaching, to comfortably pay for my Wintermester class.

—UNR Sophomore

Amy helped me with my journey to Ireland. We laid out my finances and I value what she has taught me. She taught me that finances don't have to be scary. Every meeting we laid out "to-do" lists that made getting all the things I had to get done way easier! Amy gave me a tool that I use daily. It is a financial spreadsheet that calculates and helps categorize my spending and my savings with my paychecks every month. I will continue to use it while in Ireland.

—UNR Junior

I found these sessions immensely valuable. It helped give me new ways to track my spending and income, which has been extremely effective. I was very unsure of my personal financial situation at the beginning, but now I have a very firm grip on my finances and can save money more effectively."

—UNR Recent Graduate

I always feel better about myself after I meet with you.

—UNR Freshman

NMM also focuses on key agendas such as increased partnerships with departments on campus. The success of the program is because of the cross-departmental support in both the Student Services Division as well as from others on campus. Partnerships include NevadaFIT, the Joe Crowley Student Union, Career Studio, TRiO, The Center for Student Cultural Diversity, Athletics, Alumni, Residential Life & Housing, WolfCard, WolfShop, McNair Scholars, First in the Pack, Veterans Office, Business School, ASUN, Student Ambassadors, GenFKD, the College of Science, the School of Medicine, and the College of Liberal Arts.

NMM has served approximately 8,140 students total (2,500+ in 2016, 3,340+ in 2015, & 2,300+ in 2014). The team also schedules multiple events throughout the year both on campus and in the community:

- Thirty-four point-of-contact meetings with various departments and community partners
- Thirty-one presentations
- Twenty-five tabling events
- Twenty community outreach events

And, to increase communications to students, our NMM website (unr.edu/nevada-money-mentors) allows students to explore resources on their own and schedule coaching appointments.

The money-savvy outreach on campus is improving students' money management skills; we are beginning to collect data to support that a successful financial literacy program on campus can reduce student loan debt and/or cohort default rate (CDR), improve retention, and increase annual giving and alumni engagement. The effort also aligns with wellness initiatives, increases student engagement, positions students and alumni for financial success, and increases campus-community partnerships.

Maria is now a senior at the University of Nevada, Reno. We met for financial coaching eight times over a course of a year and a half. She went to Costa Rica to study abroad. She is saving for a car. She continues to balance her academics with her work schedule. She will graduate in May 2018 and go on to achieve a master's degree in education. Having a "money mentor" helped her create a financial survival plan for college and beyond as well as improve her confidence in the way she manages money.

To ensure we have the strongest, most competitive graduates entering the workforce, we need our students to be able to manage their financial lives well (An, 2014). Our future outlook includes enriching our NMM brand, increasing staffing, establishing community partnerships and funding opportunities, and continuing to engage our students in conversations about personal finance.

Financially literate individuals have the flexibility to invest in their education, expand their businesses, and contribute to their community's economic stability (An, 2014). Nevada Money Mentors is committed to building that capability, empowering our students, and helping them each achieve not just financial success but overall success in their lives.

References

American Psychological Association. (2015). *Stress in America: Paying with our health.* Washington, DC.

An, Veronica. (2014) Colleges must encourage greater financial literacy. *Daily Trojan*, March 2, 2014, dailytrojan.com/2014/03/02/colleges-must-encourage-greater-financial-literacy.

Berkowitz, C. (2014), Financial literacy within our communities. *Council for Economic Education*, April 16, 2014, councilforeconed.org/2014/04/16/financial-literacy-within-our-communities.

Bill & Melinda Gates Foundation, Public Agenda. (2016) *With their whole lives ahead of them [Report].* Retrieved from publicagenda.org/pages/with-their-whole-lives-ahead-of-them-reality-.

Collins, J. M. & O'Rourke, C. (2013) Financial Capability Scale (FCS), University of Wisconsin Madison, *Center for Financial Security.* fyi.uwex.edu/financialcoaching/measures/.

Donkey. *Infographics: College Debt, Grades, and Alcohol.* Retrieved from http://www.creditdonkey.com/college-alcohol.html.

How to minimize debt and be successful in college. (2014). Infographic illustration Credit
McGurran, Brianna. (2018) "2018 student loan debt statistics." *NerdWallet*, 5 June
    2018, nerdwallet.com/blog/loans/student-loans/student-loan-debt.
Prosperity Now. (2017). *Assets & opportunity scorecard.* Washington, DC: State of
    Nevada Report.
Shin, Laura. (2014) 4 In 5 millennials optimistic for future, but half live paycheck to
    paycheck. *Forbes,* December 5, 2014, forbes.com/sites/laurashin/2014/12/05/4-in-
    5-millennials-optimistic-for-future-but-half-live-paycheck-to-paycheck.

CHAPTER 9

Starting Freshman on the Right Foot

Advanced Registration

THEO MEEK, MA

Theo Meek is a scholar-practitioner at the University of Nevada, Reno. In his currently role as director of advising for the University's Advising Center, he works with interdisciplinary student populations. His research interest is in the disparity amongst college preparation for first-generation college students as well as gateway course policy and development. Meek is pursuing a Ph.D. in public policy at the University of Nevada, Reno.

What do 3,183 students, a 93.2 percent full-time semester-to-semester retention rate, and an average enrollment of 15.8 credits all have in common? They are all characteristics of the freshman class of Fall 2016 that participated in the University of Nevada, Reno's Advanced Registration program.

Advanced Registration is a first-semester recruitment and matriculation tool coordinated by the Office of Admissions and Records. It is used to ensure enrollment in degree-applicable courses, reduce enrollment melt of newly admitted freshmen, and assist with new-student transition from high school. Advanced Registration partners student services with academic-advising teams to enroll all incoming freshmen into their first semester classes.

The success rate of the students who participate in Advanced Registration is remarkable. Since its full implementation in 2013, the number of students who have participated has increased. The average number of credits in which students are enrolled has also increased. Following is a breakdown of the average number of first-semester credits in which Advanced Registration students are enrolled.

Credit enrollment continued to grow in Fall 2016 with the continuation of the program. Not only have we found that students are

TABLE 9.1. Average increase in credit enrollment for students enrolled through Advanced Registration.

College	2013	2014	2015	2016
Agriculture, Biotechnology, and Natural Resources	13.4	14.5	15.3	16.0
Business	14.2	14.1	15.7	15.6
Education	14.0	14.8	15.6	15.6
Engineering	13.5	14.1	15.5	15.5
Health Sciences	13.8	14.9	15.3	15.8
Journalism	13.9	14.9	15.7	16.1
Liberal Arts	13.9	14.8	15.6	15.9
Science	13.8	14.9	15.5	16.5
Interdisciplinary	13.4	14.2	15.4	15.7
University Average	13.8	14.6	15.5	15.8

TABLE 9.2. Longitudinal review of those who participated in Advanced Registration in Fall 2016 and their sequential Spring 2017 enrollment.

College	Fall 2016	Spring 2017
Agriculture, Biotechnology, and Natural Resources	15.9	15.3
Business	15.5	14.9
Education	15.6	14.5
Engineering	15.5	15.3
Health Sciences	15.7	15.5
Journalism	16.0	15.3
Liberal Arts	15.8	15.2
Science	16.3	15.4
Interdisciplinary	15.5	15.0
University Average	15.7	14.9

enrolled in a larger number of credits during their first semester, but they also continue this momentum during their second semester.

With the importance of the Nevada System of Higher Education's (NSHE) 15-To-Finish and the University's 30-To-Complete initiatives, Advanced Registration has been the catalyst of change for the institution to swiftly adapt to the mantra that "fifteen credits is full time." Enrollment in fifteen credits has not been the only important policy

FIGURE 9.1. Percent of first-time,degree-seeking students that enrolled in math in the first year of enrollment.

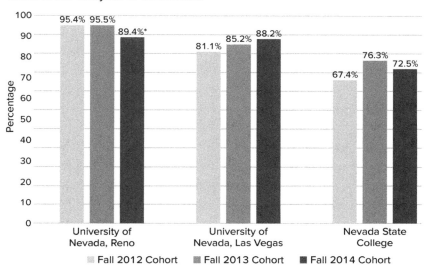

Note: Fall 2014 UNR Cohort is speculated to be smaller due to underreporting of AP/IB test credit.

to be adopted by the University. The Continuous Enrollment Policy, established by NSHE, has put immediate pressure on Nevada's colleges and universities to mandate enrollment in math and English during a first-time student's initial year. With considerable assistance from Advanced Registration, the University of Nevada, Reno has maintained the highest percentage of students enrolled in math during their first year across all colleges and universities in the state of Nevada.

The University of Nevada, Reno has seen great success because of a robust campus-wide commitment to the implementation of the Continuous Enrollment Policy.

In addition to data relating to policy implementation, Advanced Registration is also able to identify students who are first-generation, that is, students whose parent(s) have not obtained at least a bachelor's degree. Of all students who completed the Advanced Registration questionnaire, 41 percent were identified as first-generation college students. Furthermore, among Nevada high school graduates who participated, 44 percent were identified as first-generation.

TABLE 9.3. Summary of first-generation students by the University's predominant recruitment regions.

Status	Washoe County	Clark County	Other County	Nevada Total	Out of State	Grand Total
First-generation	407	425	155	987	382	1369
Non First-generation or Unknown	597	510	158	1265	705	1970
Total	1004	935	313	2252	1087	3339

Advanced Registration's successful implementation is made possible by maintaining strong relationships with our academic colleagues. Dr. Joe Cline, vice provost of undergraduate education, and Dr. Derek Furukawa, assistant vice provost of undergraduate academic advising and student achievement, have been instrumental in ensuring class availability needs are met, that course sequencing is made a priority, and that the University successfully transitions into the new Silver Core Curriculum. The Silver Core Curriculum is a recent restructuring of the general core curriculum required by all students to complete at the University.

As the institution continues to see fast-growing populations of first-generation and students of color, what is the future of Advanced Registration as a tool to support the diversification of the institution? Moreover, how can we enhance Advanced Registration and other student support services to help them matriculate?

The potential impact of Advanced Registration is limitless; corequisite remediation, developmental education, gateway course enrollment, core completion, and degree applicability are just some of the topics which the program supports.

CHAPTER 10

NevadaFIT

Bootcamps for Academic Success

KEVIN R. CARMAN, PH.D.

As the executive vice president and provost, Kevin Carman oversees the University's twelve colleges and schools, the Division of Extended Studies, and the University of Nevada Cooperative Extension. He also has responsibility for the Office of Research and Innovation, the Office of Information Technology, University Libraries, the University of Nevada Press, and KUNR. In his role as executive vice president, he serves as the University's chief executive officer when President Marc Johnson is away. Carman was appointed to his position by President Johnson in February 2013.

Most entering college freshmen, regardless of their academic credentials, do not have a clear idea of the style, pace, and intensity of college-level classes. Further, they often come to college with misperceptions about how they should interact with faculty, the importance of regularly attending class, the value and accessibility of tutoring and counseling and tutoring services, and many other foreign and sometimes confusing aspects of university life. Students who do not quickly make the necessary adjustments to college life are at risk of experiencing early failure, which may cause stress and confusion and lead to a cascading sequence of negative outcomes. When students do not perform up to their expectations, they may lose confidence and decide that they are not capable of being successful in college. They simply may decide that they are not happy in college. Regardless, a negative beginning to a college experience often leads to a student dropping out. We are confident that all students admitted to the University of Nevada, Reno are academically capable of being successful, and we sincerely *want* them to be successful. Toward that end, UNR has established NevadaFIT

(FIT="Freshman Intensive Transition"), an intensive five-day academic orientation program for entering freshmen that is designed to help students start their academic experience on a positive trajectory.

The NevadaFIT academic boot-camp concept can be traced to a program, "BIOS," a program that was established at Louisiana State University in 2005 for entering freshmen who planned to major in biology. BIOS has been recognized by national organizations such as the American Association for the Advancement of Science and the Howard Hughes Medical Institute for its positive impact on biology majors, and BIOS has been replicated at more than thirty universities nationwide. However, all of these universities have limited the program to students majoring in biology.

At UNR we have taken the BIOS model, and modified and expanded it to include students who are pursuing academic majors that span the University. The first installment of NevadaFIT was in 2013. Under the inspired leadership of Jeffrey Thompson, dean of the College of Science, and College of Science academic advisor Christina Cho, BioFIT welcomed forty-eight students who were majoring in biology and neuroscience. The program has grown each subsequent year, and in 2016 more than 970 students participated in NevadaFIT, including programs in the College of Agriculture, Biotechnology, and Natural Resources (CABNR); Business; Education; Engineering; Health Sciences; Journalism; Liberal Arts; and Science. Also, in 2016, the College of Science boldly made NevadaFIT a requirement for all entering freshmen. In 2017, CABNR will make NevadaFIT a requirement for all of its entering freshmen.

The need for NevadaFIT can be summarized using three numbers:

- *Twelve.* Students who attend college have generally been quite successful students for twelve years of grade school, middle school, and high school. While students certainly have many anxieties about going to college, for the most part they feel confident about their intellectual capacity. Many entering freshmen have not been seriously challenged in their classes and have been able to make good grades without too much effort.
- *Thirteen.* Entering freshmen tend to expect that, from an academic perspective, college will be grade thirteen. They understandably

think that study habits they have used in high school will translate seamlessly to their college classes. They are often surprised by exam questions that require them to synthesize information in ways that are new to them. They are also surprised at the pace of college courses. The amount of material that is covered in one semester is roughly equivalent to what a high-school class covers in a year. And this happens in only two or three lectures per week.

- *Eighteen.* They are, on average, eighteen years old. They are at a wonderful time in their life when they are full of confidence, and are emerging as young adults. Similar to the superheroes who wear a big red "S" on their chest, they feel invincible. Overconfidence can have very negative consequences. Students who fail to understand and adapt to the very different style, pace, and intensity of college courses may experience initial failure in classes that is very confusing and discouraging. Having never performed poorly in a class, students have a difficult time accepting that they are doing anything wrong. They are reluctant to seek assistance from tutoring centers, and they are intimidated by the notion of seeking advice from their professors. Many well-meaning students simply respond by saying "I'll work harder," but they fail to recognize that, while hard work is important, if their approach to their classes is fundamentally flawed, simply working harder will not solve the problem. And the adjustment to a very different style of learning is made all the more challenging as students adjust to a schedule that has little accountability (most professors do not take attendance) and what appears to be an enormous amount of free time (students are in a formal classroom setting only 15–18 hours per week).

In a compact and demanding five-day program, NevadaFIT is designed to give new freshmen a concrete and immediately relevant experience that will help them avoid many of the pitfalls described above. It is a one-credit-hour, pass/fail class; the only requirement for earning the credit is to fully participate in the program. In NevadaFIT, students participate in a class in which they will be enrolled in the coming fall semester. The professor who will teach the class leads the NevadaFIT courses. Lectures, homework, and exams are drawn directly from the actual class. Thus, students directly experience what the class will be like. They learn the value of preparing for class. They take exams, get feedback on their performance, and learn how to prepare for and more successfully take future exams. They are exposed to and use tutoring centers and learn the importance of time management.

Each student is placed into a group of six students within their major that we call a "Pack." Each Pack is led by an upper-class undergraduate mentor who has been successful as a UNR student. Throughout the five-day boot camp, the Pack mentor works closely with his or her students and gives them a personal tutorial on how to be a successful college student. The Pack also learns the value of studying together. When they go to class "for real" on their first day, they see several other students that they know and with whom they have developed a bond. Pack members often form lasting friendships and continue studying together when the academic year begins. Pack members also commonly form close relationships with their mentor and stay connected with them. These relationships form an important support network that helps students successfully navigate the many challenges of college life.

While a realistic classroom experience is the fundamental focus of NevadaFIT, the program exposes students to resources and best practices that will help them be successful and realize their full potential. They learn the importance of attending class and of allocating adequate time for preparing for class, projects, and examinations . . . and fun! They learn the value of and get experience using the variety of academic-support resources that are available to them, including math, writing, and tutoring centers. They learn about the availability of counseling services and how to obtain accommodations for disabilities. Students participate in group projects relevant to their major. They meet the faculty who will be teaching classes within their major, and they learn about the exciting and varied research and creative activity happening at the University. They learn how they can get involved with research as undergraduate students. They learn that their professors keep office hours and are eager to meet with them individually or in small groups to help them be successful. Students also get exposed to a variety of extracurricular activities such as clubs that can enrich their college experience.

NevadaFIT participants who will be living in a dormitory during the academic year move into their dorm room just prior to the beginning of the program. They take their meals in the University dining facilities. This allows students to begin the important process of becoming adjusted to the lifestyle and daily rhythms of college.

Collectively, the NevadaFIT schedule keeps students fully occupied from breakfast through late at night. It is a rigorous and demanding experience. When the program wraps up at noon on Thursday, students are tired, but feeling confident that they are prepared to be successful in college.

NevadaFIT requires a tremendous and coordinated effort by every aspect of University operations: administrators, faculty, and academic advisors. Staff members from residential life, dining, financial aid, the registrar, and student recruiting also play essential roles in assuring that NevadaFIT is successful. Initial planning begins in the fall semester and intensifies in the spring and summer.

While NevadaFIT may seem like a good idea, it would not be worth the considerable effort if it did not have an impact. Accordingly, we carefully track performance of NevadaFIT participants and constantly look for ways to improve the program. The results thus far are encouraging. For example, among the first group of forty-eight biology and neuroscience students who participated in NevadaFIT in 2013, 89 percent were still enrolled at UNR in Fall 2016 (their senior year!); among biology and neuroscience students who started in 2013 but did not participate in NevadaFIT, 73 percent were still enrolled at UNR. Among the 2013 cohort, NevadaFIT participants had also completed more credit hours and had a higher GPA than nonparticipants.

The program was expanded to nonscience programs in 2014, and initial results were mixed. For many programs there was no real evidence of improved retention or overall performance. We discovered that many of the programs were not focusing on the core class experience and were instead emphasizing group projects and social activities. Significant program changes were made for 2015, the most notable of which was the use of math classes to anchor most NevadaFIT programs. Math classes appear to be the "secret sauce" for NevadaFIT programs. Students participating in a NevadaFIT math class had much higher grades and completion rates in their math classes, regardless of whether they were in introductory math or advanced calculus. Across all 2015 programs, 89 percent of NevadaFIT students returned for their sophomore year, significantly greater than the institutional average of 82 percent.

Collectively we have very good evidence that NevadaFIT has a highly positive impact on students. It gets them started immediately on a favorable trajectory in college and initiates a virtuous cycle of success that persists throughout their college career. It benefits all students, from National Merit Scholars to those who barely meet admission requirements. NevadaFIT has a particularly positive influence on students who are the first in their immediate family to attend college, and on students who have modest financial resources.

Following on these observations, it is imperative that NevadaFIT be available to all students, regardless of their background or financial capacity. Accordingly, we provide financial assistance to students with need to offset both the cost of the course and dormitory. We identify students with need and reach out to them through various media to encourage them to participate and to be sure they know that financial assistance is available. We are able to provide this assistance because of the private gifts provided by many individuals, charitable foundations, and companies.

The University of Nevada, Reno is a special place for many reasons. It is a vibrant, beautiful research university with state-of-the-art facilities and world-class faculty. UNR faculty and staff are deeply committed to student success and they demonstrate it in many tangible ways. The institution is known as a place with a heart and soul, as well as a place with exceptional scholarly programs. Our overarching objective is to maintain and continue to elevate our reputation as a world-class research university, and to provide every opportunity for students to excel and achieve at the highest level. NevadaFIT is one important way through which UNR demonstrates its ongoing commitment to excellent scholarship and student success.

CHAPTER 11

TRiO Scholars

Overcoming Obstacles and Finding Support

DANIEL VALLE, PH.D.

The associate director of the TRiO Scholars Program at the University of
Nevada, Reno, Daniel Valle graduated from the University of Oregon with a degree in ethnic studies. He went on to teach in public schools in Baltimore, where
he earned a master's degree in teaching from Johns Hopkins University. He later
earned another master's degree in international management from Whitworth
University in eastern Washington, where he studied organizational behavior and
worked for various nonprofits. He moved to the Reno area in 2006 and began
teaching in the Washoe County School District for six years. In 2012 he became
the assistant director of the TRiO Scholars Program at the University of Nevada,
Reno. He recently received a doctorate degree in education.

For low-income, first-generation students (LIFG), gaining access to a
college education is a continuous challenge. Many students who identify as LIFG view institutions of higher learning as something foreign.
"For many first-generation, low-income students college is an unknown
land at which they dream of arriving one distant day" (Jehangir, 2009,
p. 33). Low-income, first-generation students who end up attending a
four-year institution are twice as likely as students whose parents hold
a bachelor's degree to drop out before their second year (Yeh, 2010).
"[First-generation students] are 71 percent more likely to drop out of
college than [non first-generation students], even after controlling for
race, gender, high school grade point average, and family income"
(Ishitani 2003, as cited in Prospero & Vohra-Gupta, 2007, p. 964). This
creates a significant gap between the students who are well on their
way to earning a degree and those who are not. More specifically, the
gap exists between those who are on a graduation path and those who

feel lost as college students. This gap separates those students who reap the benefits of a college education in comparison to those who do not complete their degree. In Bragg, Kim, and Barnett's (2006) work, the authors reference previous studies that note students who do not enter or remain in college do not experience the same benefits of a degree, such as increased annual earnings, as college graduates (Howe, 1988; Rosenbaum, 2001, in Bragg, Kim, & Barnett, 2006).

As one of the fastest-growing student populations on college campuses (Tinto, 2012), LIFGs command the attention of college faculty and administrators. "First-generation college students are becoming more visible on campuses, and researchers have demonstrated a vested interest in understanding this unique student group given distinct challenges they may face" (Garriott et al., 2015, p. 253). With a growing number of LIFG students enrolling in college, campuses are seeing a cultural shift from the previous norm of continued-generation college students who require few resources and complete a degree in four years. LIFGs are realizing the importance of earning a college degree. Research shows economic issues are also contributing factors to this cultural shift in institutions of higher education. "Due to the economic and social costs of *not* achieving a bachelor's degree, universities have seen increases in enrollments of historically underrepresented students, including first-generation college students" (Engle et al., as cited in Garriott et al., 2015).

Research also suggests LIFGs tend to be extremely hard-working (both on campus and off campus), oftentimes supporting themselves in school (Byrd, 2001). Additionally, a growing number of LIFG students are participating in extracurricular activities on campus. They gain personally and academically from these experiences. "Extracurricular involvement had stronger positive effects on critical thinking, degree plans, sense of control over (and responsibility for) their own academic success, and preference for higher-order cognitive tasks for first-generation than for other students" (Pascarella et al., 2004, p. 278). LIFGs see the value in participating in extracurricular activities.

Another point to consider is the way LIFGs reflect some of the population numbers of the cities in which colleges and universities are established. Since LIFG students are more likely to stay in the town in which they live to attend college (rather than seek to enroll in an out-of-state institution), they represent, to a degree, a picture of the local diversity of the campus town (Mudge & Higgins, 2011). As stated earlier, LIFGs truly reflect the changing demographics in the United States (Jehangir, 2010). Finally, LIFG students who persist in school bring a sense of resiliency when it comes to learning and completing a degree. "[LIFG] students who persisted in college appeared to be sufficiently resilient that these disadvantages did not necessarily translate into a parallel pattern of disadvantages in cognitive and noncognitive outcomes" (Pascarella et al., 2004, p. 277). This indicates that LIFG students often must overcome several issues or challenges as college students.

Social Challenges

Social issues, or in many cases, social challenges, play an important part in the success (or lack of success) of LIFG students. These social issues include, but are not limited to, understanding the norms and expectations of a college or university; finding the right support while in school; and facing the burden of being the first member of the family to pursue a college education (Bragg, Kim, & Barnett, 2006). Much like other areas of education, social challenges have many layers. To this point, the research on LIFG students focuses on two aspects of social challenges: social and cultural challenges, and family challenges. Both have a tremendous effect on the lives of LIFG students.

Social and cultural issues are related to the culture of the university as well as the social and cultural capital LIFG students possess (or may not possess) once they enroll (Bergerson, 2009). Housel and Harvey (2011) address these issues of culture within an institution of higher learning. "They [LIFG students] must often navigate the unwritten social rules of their peers, professors, and academic administrators, many of whom come from middle- and upper-class backgrounds" (Lubrano, 2004 as cited in Housel & Harvey, 2011, p. 6). The authors suggest that all incoming students must understand certain unwritten rules within a university—a skill that the low-income, first-generation student population may not have.

Additionally, much like the social and cultural issues addressed above, the family also plays a key role in the social challenges LIFG students face in higher education. The literature touches on the influence that families have on LIFGs and, consequently, their success in school. "It is not uncommon that many first-generation students (FGs) feel the tensions of entering new territory and that their parents are unable to reassure or support them appropriately," (Unverferth el al., 2012, p. 240). This tension and lack of support can be detrimental to a college student. Aside from these issues, many LIFGs face some sort of cultural shock, leaving their own culture at home while trying to adapt to a new culture at school. Miller addresses this issue in his research: "Cultural change is a problem encountered by first-generation students regarding the discomforts that arise upon leaving the social standing of one's family of orientation," (Miller, 2007, p. 31). This cultural shock demonstrates the importance of assisting LIFG students on campus—assuring them that they are capable of overcoming these social challenges.

The Effect of Colleges and Universities on LIFGs

It is important to consider how colleges and universities see this growing population on their campuses, since LIFG students are among the least likely to be retained through degree completion (Thayer, 200). LIFG students face several social barriers in higher education. Colleges and universities are aware of these barriers and continuously look for ways to address them with this student population. Thayer (2000) states that, though colleges and universities have educational goals (graduation rates) and institutional goals (bringing in funds, increasing research), they are also interested in increasing access to LIFG students. There is a reason for this increased interest and commitment to LIFG students. Conley and Hamlin (2009), in their study of efficacy with LIFG students, examined a semester-long, first-year seminar course that taught students about social justice and service learning. From this course, the researchers interviewed and observed three participants for their study—looking at both academics and service learning. In their findings, the researchers noted that "higher education continually attempts to identify effective means for engaging and retaining traditionally marginalized populations, particularly first-generation college students of color from low-income backgrounds." (Conley & Hamlin, 2009, p. 47).

Conversely, there are researchers who believe that colleges are not doing enough for this student population. Gray (2013) suggests that, though institutions of higher learning are seeing a demand from LIFGs, they struggle to connect with this student population and may not focus too much on their retention rates. "Universities attend to recruiting students from local high schools, often cultivating a demand from first-generation, low-income students, and students of color—but often without investing much effort into insuring the success or graduation of students they admit," (Gray, 2013, p. 1245). In both cases, the literature suggests institutions of higher learning must continue to find ways of reaching LIFG students and making sure they do not feel vulnerable or as outsiders (Pyne & Means, 2013).

In addition to the institutional view of this ever-growing student population, research shows the need for effective strategies that are taking place (or should be taking place) in higher education. First, it is important to consider how effective the role of mentors can be when working with LIFGs, since studies suggest that students who interact with university personnel are more satisfied with their academic experiences (Bruce et al., 1982 as cited in Wallace et al., 2000). Second, as it pertains to the efforts of colleges and universities, the author will also outline the importance of retention programs. Institutions that employ retention programs have seen gains in retention and graduation numbers. What follows is a review of the way colleges and universities respond to the increasing number of LIFG students and the importance of retention programs on college campuses.

How Higher Education See LIFGs

Despite the multiple challenges that LIFG students may face, the dynamic between students and campus administrators and faculty is also an important variable that impacts the student's journey through higher education. More importantly, how do institutions view and engage LIFG students?

Research studies show that there is a growing interest in low-income, first-generation student persistence amongst colleges and universities. Bergerson (2009) states: "Changing demographics across the United States lead to a call for a renewed commitment to equity in higher education, and many programs ... seek to increase the participation of under-represented students in postsecondary education" (p. 85). Thayer (2000) states that, though colleges and universities have educational goals (graduation rates) and institutional goals (bringing in funds, increasing research), institutions of higher learning are also interested in increasing access to LIFG students. There is a reason for this increased interest and commitment to LIFG students. According to Gray (2013), colleges and universities are failing in their efforts to graduate this population of students. Gray further points out that the responsibility falls on all members of the institution to make sure that LIFGs succeed in higher education. "The entire campus community must be involved in coordinated programs that address both academic and nonacademic factors in an integrated manner" (Gray, 2013, p. 1249). One variable that has a direct effect on student persistence is the quality of relationships with significant members of the college community (Heisserer & Parette, 2002). For these reasons, it is important to consider the role of the entire institution of higher learning—professors, administrators, support staff, student services—as it relates to LIFG students.

Faculty and Staff Getting Involved

The growth of LIFG numbers on campus has put an onus on faculty and staff to be more hands-on with their students. From an LIFG student's viewpoint, having faculty and staff members being "hands on" with them may not seem like a regular occurrence. In a 1996 study Terenzini, Pascarella et al. (2004) note that LIFGs were less likely to notice that faculty on campus were concerned about students. In their 2015 study, Garriott et al. observe that LIFG students oftentimes experience cultural mismatches with the established norms of college environments, thus struggling with institutional policies. For these reasons, supporting this student population, and personally meeting their needs, is crucial for their overall success. "Environmental supports, both on and off-campus, have been identified as critical to first-generation college students' success and overall well-being." (Garriott et al., 2015, p. 254). Further, the researchers show that, as noted above, the increased presence of LIFG students force administrative and academic faculty members to work with this population. They suggest colleges and universities should either develop or fund systematic plans and resources to connect LIFG students with support specialists on campus, or possibly reach out to important people in students' lives (2015). Those campus administrators and faculty members who choose to engage, and spend time with, LIFG students notice how building a relationship with them benefits all parties involved. "An understanding of first-generation students will allow for more focused recruiting, program development, retention, and graduation efforts," (Inman & Mayes, 1996, p. 3). Lastly, research shows students who participate in some sort of collaborative work with faculty on campus are more likely to succeed. In his study, Ishiyama (2012) suggests students who participate in collaborative research early in their educational careers perform better academically (Ishiyama, 2002). The author claims students who participated in research with academic faculty benefited overall from their experiences. The strengths which low-income, first-generation students bring to an institution of higher learning in terms of tenacity, resiliency, hard work, and a willingness to participate on campus, combined with the efforts of dedicated faculty and staff, have shown to be a successful marriage with beneficial outcomes.

LIFGs and the University of Nevada, Reno

The Fall 2014 undergraduate enrollment of citizens and eligible non-citizens at the University of Nevada, Reno (UNR) was 15,635; nearly 40 percent qualify as first-generation. Only 22 percent of Nevadans have a bachelor's degree or above, a reality that significantly contributes to the large number of first-generation students on campus. In addition, added to these alarming statistics is the fact that in 2014, Nevada had the nation's second-highest U.S. unemployment rate (Bureau of Labor Statistics, 2014). Nevada is also clawing its way back from the country's highest foreclosure rate. Parents of eligible students are likely among the high number of Nevadans either out of work or seriously underemployed. About half of UNR undergraduates (48 percent) are eligible for need-based aid (Financial Aid Report, 2014). While only 13 percent of UNR students received Pell grants in 2009, by Spring 2014, that figure jumped to 30 percent. UNR is home to a high, and growing, number of low-income students.

Connecting to Campus Resources

Many freshmen do not use University support services. For example, only 25 percent of students accessing walk-in labs for math and science received Pell Grants (UNR Tutoring Center Report, 2014). Yet nearly 40 percent of UNR freshmen reported feeling under prepared for one or more of their courses (Your First College Year, 2014). More than 50 percent of incoming freshman students reported that they sometimes go to class without completing assignments. Almost 40 percent also reported they are not participating in student clubs or groups (NSSE, 2013). Freshmen are not making use of the academic and other resources available at UNR. A need exists for a structured program to facilitate the college transition of first-year students, including familiarization with support services and connection to clubs and organizations.

TRiO Programs

As noted above, creating and nurturing critical relationships on campus can be vital to the success of first-generation, income-qualified students, many of whom are Latino students. Since the creation of positive relationships on campus has been documented in this chapter, it is necessary to address mentoring, retention, and support networks already in place on college campuses. What follows is a brief review of these networks and programs, with an emphasis on TRiO federally-funded programs, as they share a common thread amongst college and universities throughout the United States.

TRiO Student Support Services (SSS) is a program that assists LIFG students. "TRiO programs exist for students . . . desiring higher education, but needing guidance through the academic systems that exist" (Graham, 2011, p. 33). Started in the 1960s by the United States Department of Education to facilitate the development of mentoring relationships in higher education, TRiO SSS works to ensure that students stay in college until they earn their baccalaureate degree (Wallace, Ropers-Huilman, & Abel, 2000). Programs such as TRiO SSS assist in increasing the retention and graduation rates of LIFG students. They target this student population because they are "already at a disadvantage when starting college, beginning their journey with less academic preparation, less financial and informational resources from parents, and lack of understanding of how to successfully navigate through college life," (Mamiseishvili, 2000, p. 66). Furthermore, there are certain components—academic preparation, mentoring, nurturing aspirations, and financial assistance— that are part of an effective college program, according to Bergerson (2009). "Those who can address most if not all of these components will have the greatest impact on bringing down the many barriers standing in the way of postsecondary education for students of color and low socioeconomic status," (Bergerson, 2009, p. 97). Additionally, Wallace, Ropers-Huilman, and Abel (2004) note that since LIFG students face barriers which inhibit their ability to enter and succeed in a program of postsecondary education, intrusive advising and other support programs are instrumental in the success of students from backgrounds that have not historically been well served by higher education. Overall, the primary goal of federal TRiO programs is to increase postsecondary academic success, retention, and graduation of first-generation, low-income students and students with disabilities (Wallace, Ropers-Huilman, & Abel, 2000).

Outcomes for Student Support

The TRiO Scholars (SSS) program has pledged to assist a minimum of 75 percent of its participants to persist from one year to the next. Although participants are selected based on first-generation and low-income eligibility, at least 75 percent will be retained because of targeted services provided through the SSS program. In addition to persisting from one academic year to the next, it is imperative that program participants also maintain satisfactory academic standing in order to stay eligible for financial aid, to gain entrance into major programs of study, and to stay on track for timely graduation. A minimum of 85 percent of participants will maintain good academic standing (2.0 GPA or higher and meet PACE requirements for completing 70 percent of credits attempted) from one academic year to the next. The cost of attending UNR is significant for eligible students. To mitigate the cost, it is necessary that program services result in the shortest possible time to graduation. Therefore, a minimum of 50 percent of program participants will graduate within six years despite the considerable academic and other needs that threaten to derail their progress to graduation.

Conclusion

The need for support services for LIFG students in higher education remains critical. The TRiO Scholars Program believes that students from all socioeconomic levels should have equal opportunity to obtain a postsecondary education. The TRiO Scholars program is a "multidimensional program which provides academic support, supplemental study groups, learning communities, and leadership development for first-generation college students" (Jehangir, 2008, p. 35). TRiO programs, according to Graham (2011), provide academic and social knowledge that can shape students, helping them become engaged learners. Through their work, TRiO practitioners are able to help LIFG students overcome those academic, class, and social barriers, and to succeed in higher education.

References

Bergerson, A. (2009). College preparation programs. *ASHE Higher Education Report,* 35(4), 85–97.

Bragg, D., Kim, E. Barnett, E. (2006) Creating access and success: Academic pathways reaching underserved students. *New Directions for Community Colleges,* 1(135), 5–19.

Conley, P. A., & Hamlin, M. L. (2009). Justice-learning: Exploring the efficacy with low-income, first-generation college students. *Michigan Journal Of Community Service Learning,* 16(1), 47–58.

Garriott, P. O., Hudyma, A., Keene, C., & Santiago, D. (2015). Social cognitive predictors of first- and non-first-generation college students' academic and life satisfaction. *Journal of Counseling Psychology,* 62(2), 253–263.

Graham, L. (2011). Learning a new world: Reflections on being a first-generation college student and the influence of TRiO programs. *New Directions for Teaching and Learning,* (127), 33–39.

Gray, S (2013). Framing "at risk" students: Struggles at the boundaries of access to higher education. *Children and Youth Services Review* 35(8), 1245–1251

Housel, T. H., & Harvey, V. L. (2011). Introduction: Shall we gather in the classroom? *New Directions for Teaching and Learning,* (127), 5–10.

Ishiyama, J. (2002). Does early participation in undergraduate research benefit social science and humanities students? *College Student Journal,* 36(3), 380–386.

Jehangir, R. R. (2009). Cultivating voice: First-generation students seek full academic citizenship in multicultural learning communities. *Innovative Higher Education*, 34(1), 33–49.

Jehangir, R. (2010). Stories as knowledge: Bringing the lived experience of first-generation college students into the academy. *Urban Education*, 45(4), 533–553.

Mamiseishvili, K. (2010). Effects of employment on persistence of low-income, first-generation college students. *College Student Affairs Journal*, 29(1), 65–74.

Miller, B. R. (2007). The association of family history knowledge and cultural change with persistence among college students. *Framework*, 24(1), 29–46.

Mudge, S., & Higgins, D. J. (2011). College access programming: Removing higher education barriers for underrepresented student populations. *International Journal of Learning*, 17(11), 123–140.

Pascarella, E. T., Pierson, C. T., Wolniak, G. C., & Terenzini, P. T. (2004). First-generation college students. *Journal of Higher Education*, 75(3), 249–284.

Próspero, M., & Vohra-Gupta, S. (2007). First-generation college students: Motivation, integration, and academic achievement. *Community College Journal of Research and Practice*, 31(12), 963–975.

Thayer, P. (2000). Retention of students from first-generation and low-income backgrounds. *Journal of the Counsel for Opportunity in Education.*, 9. Retrieved from http://www.TRiOprograms.org/clearinghouse.

Tinto, V. (2012). *Completing college: Rethinking institutional action*. Chicago: University of Chicago Press.

Unverferth, A., Talbert-Johnson, C., & Bogards, T. (2012). Percieved barriers for FG students. *International Journal of Education Reform*, 21(4), 238–252.

Wallace, D., Abel, R., & Ropers-Huilman, B. (2000). Clearing a path for success: Deconstructing borders through undergraduate mentoring. *The Review of Higher Education*, 24(1), 87–102.

Wallace, D. D., Ropers-Huilman, B., & Abel, R. (2004). Working in the margins: A study of university professionals serving marginalized student populations. *Journal of Student Affairs Research and Practice*, 41(3), 569–588.

Yeh, T. L. (2010). Service-learning and persistence of low-income, first-generation college students: An exploratory study. *Michigan Journal of Community Service Learning Spring*, 50–65.

CHAPTER 12

First in the Pack

DESIRAE ACOSTA, MA

Desirae Acosta is an alumna-practitioner at the University of Nevada, Reno, working in the Academic Opportunity and Support Programs office, where she works with first-generation students, focusing on their transition to college and assisting them in overcoming challenges they may face.

Defining First-Generation Students

The United States Department of Education defines first-generation students as students who are the first members of their families to attend college (2005). However, the more widely used definition for first-generation students is someone whose parents have not completed a college degree (Petty, 2014). The Nevada First in the Pack program recognizes students whose parents *or* legal guardians did not obtain a bachelor's degree.

First in the Pack

The Academic and Opportunity Support Programs (AOSP) office has housed TRiO programs such as McNair Scholars and the Student Support Services since 1967. The TRiO programs combined serve about 205 students annually. As the number of first-generation students at the University of Nevada, Reno increased, there was an apparent need for more support. In response, AOSP established the Nevada First in the Pack program in 2014. The program was modeled after TRiO's Student Support Services and guides first-generation freshmen throughout their first year of college through one-on-one meetings, workshops, and socials. Once students apply, they receive support from the First in the Pack Retention Specialist over the summer, ensuring they are enrolled in the right number of credits to receive financial aid, have information on summer opportunities, and obtain answers to any questions they and their family may have.

Coaching

Once a student is accepted into the program, they are contacted by the First in the Pack staff over the summer to address actions they can take immediately that will prepare them for the fall semester. This includes the Summer Freshmen Start program through the 365 Learning office, which allows new freshmen to take up to six credits for free during the first or second session. This is especially helpful for students who are in remedial classes. If a student in remedial classes does not participate in Summer Freshmen Start, they are also encouraged to take the AC-CUPLACER tests. Students are also notified of the NevadaFIT deadlines and the benefits of attending. Reaching out to students over the summer builds the relationship with students sooner and creates a proactive culture. Once the semester starts, each student is paired with a coach whom they meet every other week. The one-on-one meetings build a strong relationship through academic and personal coaching, giving students a go-to person for all their questions. Although each coach may not be able to answer *every* question, they are well-informed about the campus and community and are able to at least lead students to the right person who can assist them. The meeting curriculum coincides with the academic calendar, addressing challenges students may face and answering questions students may not know they need to be asking. The meetings also combat academic and personal challenges from homesickness to time management and the new academic rigor compared to high school.

The meetings provide an opportunity for students to set measurable goals and track academic progress through faculty reports and benchmarks. The support in personal development skills such as professionalism and civic engagement are supplemental to the meeting curriculum. The coaching relationship is intended to support the students in their first year of college so that they may have the skills and necessary awareness of resources to be successful in completing their bachelor's degree.

Workshops

First in the Pack provides workshops for students to receive in-depth information on college success such as completing the FAFSA, stress management, and job or internship preparedness.

Every workshop is hosted in collaboration with a different office on campus. This introduces students to the vast resources on campus and presents a familiar face so the intimidation of seeking each resource on their own is conquered. Collaborating with different resources on campus has also served as a light bulb for the professionals on campus, allowing them to brainstorm the different ways their resources can better serve and be accessible to first-generation students. For example, after speaking to our students, the Nevada Money Mentors program noticed an increase in student appointments with a financial coach. The financial coach set up a week of meetings reserved specifically for our students and followed up with them via email. After successful attendance to the meetings, both offices are working together to improve outreach to first-generation students who will clearly utilize the resource once they are made more aware of the service.

Program Outcomes

The outcomes of the first-year pilot suggested promising outcomes: 87 percent of the 2014 cohort enrolled for Fall 2015; 77 percent of the original 2014 cohort was enrolled for Fall 2016 as compared to only 49 percent of the comparison group. The 2015–2016 participants served during the second year of the program's existence enrolled for the following fall semester in impressive numbers with 90 percent retention. This outcome is just nine percentage points below that of the more robustly funded TRiO Scholars Program and nine percentage points *above* the UNR freshman retention rate of 81 percent. The 2017–2018 First in the Pack cohort Fall 2018 enrollment rate is twenty-two percentage points above the enrollment rate for students who were recruited for the program but did not participate. Program participants also earned a significantly higher cumulative GPA (3.13) than that earned by the comparison group (2.75). Among the 2017–2018 cohort, 91.5 percent enrolled in fifteen credits in the spring semester and 95 percent of those students enrolled in fifteen credits completed all fifteen credits. The 2017–2018 cohort ended the academic year with a 3.13 average GPA, and 89 percent of the students are enrolled in courses for the Fall 2018 semester.

Conclusion

With one-on-one coaching, knowledge of resources and specific work-shops, First in the Pack students have consistently performed better than students who are eligible to be in the program but were not. The success seen among the participants of First in the Pack is telling of first-generation students' potential. With continued support, First in the Pack can serve more first-generation students, students who are capable of academic success, students who *will* graduate from the University of Nevada, Reno.

References

Chen, X., & Carroll, C., D. (July 2005). *First-generation students in postsecondary education: A look at their college transcripts.* Retrieved from https://nces.ed.gov/das/epubs/pdf/2005171_es.pdf.

CHAPTER 13

College of Science's Golden Scholars Program

CHRISTINA Y. CHO, PH.D. and ERICK HENDRIXSON

Christina Cho served as the director of advising, recruitment, and retention for the College of Science at the University of Nevada, Reno from 2004–2017. Her commitment to college student success and to the creation of innovative programs yielded significant increases to the college's overall undergraduate and underrepresented minority student populations along with retention and graduation rates.

A native of Southern California, Erick Hendrixson relocated to Reno in 2015 to serve in higher education administration and to pursue his graduate studies. As a first-generation student himself, Hendrixson has a unique passion to assist other first-generation students in navigating through the diverse educational requirements toward graduation. He earned a bachelor of arts degree in strategic communications from National University, San Diego and is currently completing a master of arts in educational leadership at the University of Nevada, Reno.

Introduction

Students graduating from high school are pursuing a postsecondary education more than ever. Earning a college degree has now become "a prerequisite for access to jobs with employer-provided benefits" (Carnevale, 2007, p. 16). Additionally, our country faces a shortage of nearly one million STEM (Science, Technology, Engineering, and Mathematics) college graduates for its workforce over the next decade (PCAST, 2012). Yet, college graduation rates have declined for the last decade (Talbert, 2012). About 59 percent of first-time, full-time freshmen complete college to earn their baccalaureate degrees within a six-year period (National Center for Education Statistics, 2011).

Student retention has been a high priority for higher education for the last several decades. Tinto (2006) described it as a "heightened focus on the part of institutions . . . on increasing the rate at which students persist and graduate" (p. 2). Another reason student retention and persistence are a concern is the prospect of the federal government's consideration of "using institutional retention rates in a national system of higher educational accountability" (Tinto, 2006, p. 5). Although there has been extensive research on the issue of student retention in the last forty years, the retention and attrition rates remained unchanged (Xu, 2015).

College of Science at the University of Nevada, Reno

The University of Nevada, Reno is committed to student success. In the last decade, the academic affairs and student services divisions have developed and implemented policies and programs intended to increase the retention and graduation rates. Some examples include: (a) enrollment in a minimum number of course credits/units each term for financial aid and scholarship eligibility; (b) mandatory academic advising for a minimum of two semesters for all first-time, full-time freshmen; (c) summer orientation programs; (d) academic or college-themed living learning communities in the residence halls; (e) first-year seminar courses; and (f) freshmen intensive transition programs, known as FIT programs.

The College of Science at the University of Nevada, Reno is one of four STEM academic colleges; it offers fourteen undergraduate majors ranging from the life sciences, natural and physical sciences, mathematics, to earth sciences/earth-based engineering. Through various college specific programs and policies, the college has experienced a steady increase in its first-time, full-time freshmen. The goal is to increase retention rates and overall student success. Examples include: (a) a minimum of three semesters of mandatory academic advising for its new first-time, full-time freshmen; (b) two living learning communities in partnership with the Office of Residential Life, Housing and Food Service; (c) SCI 110, a one-credit, pass/fail graded first-year seminar course taught by a faculty member from the student's home academic department; and (d) ScienceFIT, the college's intensive academic-orientation program for incoming freshmen, which is offered the week prior to the start of the fall term. Incoming freshmen with declared majors in the College of Science are required to participate in the ScienceFIT program.

Retaining and graduating STEM students to adequately supply and fulfill the pipeline of STEM-related jobs continues to be a challenge. Chen and Solder (2013) found that approximately 48 percent of bachelor's degree-seeking students who had declared a science, technology, engineering, or mathematics (STEM) major from 2003 to 2009 had left those disciplines by the Spring 2009. Therefore, it is imperative that there are specific retention efforts and initiatives for STEM students.

Golden Scholars Program

The College of Science's Golden Scholars program was created in Spring 2016 and is a partnership with the University of Nevada, Reno's First in the Pack program. The first Golden Scholars cohort began in Fall 2016 with forty-three participants. The University's First in the Pack program was established in 2014 to serve new freshmen who self-identified as being first- generation. Joining efforts with the First in the Pack program allowed Golden Scholars participants to have access to a wide array of services, resources, and opportunities and is an example of a successful collaboration between the academic affairs and student services divisions.

For the purposes of the Golden Scholars and the First in the Pack programs, the definition of a first-generation college student was established as a student with neither parent earning a baccalaureate degree from a four-year college or university. It should come as no surprise that students with little to no guidance from their parents have some of the largest barriers to succeed in obtaining a four-year degree. According to Engle and Tinto (2008), "First-generation students were nearly four times more likely to leave higher education institutions without a degree when compared to their counterparts" (Engle & Tinto, 2008). Additionally, first-generation students struggle in higher education as a result of preexisting barriers prior to entering college. Examples of barriers include (a) the lack of knowledge in navigating the ins and outs of higher education because other family members are unable to give students proper direction; (b) the lack of finances to pay for education because many students come from low-income families that are unable to fund a college education; (c) the lack of understanding and/or awareness of available financial resources, such as the Free Application for Student Financial Aid (FASFA) and verification processes; and (d) the lack of support from their family because they want the student to be employed to help support the ongoing needs of the family (Petty, 2014).

First-generation students are generally less psychologically prepared for college (Hicks, 2003). Trying to navigate the culture of higher education alone can cause a student to become overwhelmed and to leave the university to enter the workforce or to pursue an alternative educational or vocational program. Furthermore, a first-generation student who is encouraged to attend college and enrolls in classes may still need to find paid work. Juggling and balancing work and school schedules while also trying to adjust to the increased expectations and academic rigor can leave a student feeling overwhelmed and stressed.

With such a variety of barriers for first-generation students and the need to produce more STEM graduates, the College of Science's Golden Scholars program, in partnership with the University's First in the Pack program, is designed to help new freshmen who are first-generation students with declared majors in the College of Science. The Golden Scholars and First in the Pack programs address many of these issues and challenges faced by first-generation new freshmen, such as providing assistance with the financial aid process, making appropriate referrals to campus resources, and negotiating the transition from high school to college.

Recruitment

All incoming College of Science freshmen who indicate on the University's online Advanced Registration questionnaire that neither parent has completed a baccalaureate degree are notified in several ways about the Golden Scholars program and are invited to participate by completing the online registration form for the University's First in the Pack program. First, an email invitation is sent from the dean of the College of Science which shares information about the program, followed by a recorded voice message from the dean inviting students to participate in the program. A postcard with a brief description and overview, resources, and the URL for the online registration for the University's First in the Pack program is also mailed to each student. Students with declared majors in the College of Science who completed the online registration form were sent an email to confirm their participation in the program.

Program Activities

The Golden Scholars participate in the First in the Pack orientation retreat in August and in the winter retreat in January. At the orientation retreat in August, the College of Science dean welcomes and reviews the program's purpose and goals. Golden Scholars peer mentors are also introduced, and the two books all Golden Scholars will read and discuss with their peer mentor throughout the fall semester are distributed. The two books this year were *A Mind for Numbers* by Barbara Oakley, Ph.D. and *Strengthsfinders 2.0* by Tom Rath.

A Mind for Numbers was selected because: (a) the author is from a STEM field and shares her struggle with being successful in math and science classes; (b) she relates practical information about metacognition, which includes tips on how to learn and how to overcome learning challenges; and (c) there are vignettes from students and faculty who provide tips for success and overcoming challenges/difficulties.

Higher education has begun to utilize a *strengths-based* approach in a variety of educational contexts, including in academic advising (Schreiner & Anderson, 2005; Soria & Stubblefield, 2014). *Strengthsfinders 2.0* was selected because it served a critical role in the strengths-based advising program offered to Golden Scholars, which will be discussed further.

Golden Scholars participants sign up for weekly half-hour meetings with a mentor alternating between the Golden Scholars and First in the Pack. In the fall semester, the College of Science hosts a networking/etiquette dinner for Golden Scholars. This is an opportunity for Golden Scholars to network with administrators, department chairs, faculty, and some administrators from the Division of Student Services. An etiquette expert facilitates the event, which includes a reception and a formal dinner. The etiquette expert educates Golden Scholars on important soft skills and tips on appropriate attire to appear knowledgeable, confident, and successful.

In the spring semester, the College of Science hosts a panel of leaders from the community and industries to share their stories and to answer questions from the Golden Scholars. Finally, the College of Science hosts an end-of-the-academic year celebratory banquet for the Golden Scholars featuring a keynote speaker who is either a first-generation student and/or from the STEM field.

Golden Scholar Peer Mentor

The Golden Scholar peer mentor is a student leadership role in the College of Science and is a paid position. The First in the Pack program is involved in the Golden Scholar peer mentor recruitment and selection process. Candidates for the Golden Scholar peer mentor role are current sophomores, juniors, or seniors with a declared major in the College of Science who were First in the Pack and Golden Scholars program participants themselves as first-year students. Golden Scholar peer mentors commit to working about forty hours a month; this entails up to fifteen hours of individual biweekly meetings with their mentees and up to five hours for administrative tasks and preparation for future meetings.

Strengths-Based Academic Advising

Background on StrengthsFinder 2.0

The premise of the book is that most individuals are taught to focus on improving their weaknesses to become a more competitive candidate in the job market. Therefore, people invest much of their energy, efforts, and time into improving their weaknesses. Inevitably, this results in the minimization of how to best leverage their existing strengths. How are individuals supposed to develop and excel, if those skills and talents are never recognized or fully developed? Strengthsfinder 2.0 was developed to identify people's natural talents and strengths and to encourage investing more time and energy in developing them. The online, in-depth self-assessment tool identifies the user's natural talents and outlines strengths. After users have identified their strengths, the next step is to create a strength-based action plan that develops and incorporates the top five themes generated.

Role of Academic Advising in Retention

Tinto (1987) argued that academic advising is viewed as a central component in an institution's efforts for retaining students. Ender noted that academic advising helps develop a very important relationship between the student and the advisor (as cited in Schreiner & Anderson, 2005). Furthermore, Ender asserted that academic advisors not only help build class schedules and give program advice, but they help students understand themselves, set attainable short-term and long-term goals, and learn essential decision-making skills (as cited in Schreiner & Anderson, 2005). For the academic advisor to assist students in meeting these goals, the advisor needs to implement ways for the student to make a meaningful connection to campus life. The best way to help students make this connection is to assist them in meeting their basic needs. Petty (2014) explained how Maslow's Hierarchy of Needs related to college students. There are five levels of students' needs: physiological, safety, social, esteem, and self-actualization (Petty, 2014). Through the services provided by academic advisors, students learn to build the bridges and relationships to campus, which can result in a greater probability of the student continuing their studies the following year.

Strengths-Based Advising

Schreiner and Anderson (2005) proposed a new approach to academic advising called *strengths-based advising,* which focuses on the areas of strengths and talent. This approach enables advisors to identify and build on the inherent talents students bring into the college and university setting, teaching students to develop and apply their strengths to new and challenging learning tasks. This explicit focus on students' natural talents builds the confidence and motivation necessary for achievement and persistence in college (pp. 20–21).

This approach allows advisors to assist a broader and more diverse group of students in reaching their potential and achieving excellence (Schreiner & Anderson, 2005). This style gives students the guidance and encouragement to apply their strengths to new challenging tasks and help them gain the confidence. Therefore, strengths-based advising is more effective in meeting student needs than are traditional academic advising practices.

Framework for College of Science Golden Scholars Strengths-Based Advising Process

There are four phases of the College of Science Golden Scholars strengths-based advising process completed during the fall semester:

- Golden Scholars complete the Strengthsfinder 2.0 online assessment and discuss the results with their Golden Scholar peer mentor;
- Golden Scholars reflect upon how to develop tangible ways to use their strengths in college and develop a plan that incorporates available campus resources and networking events; the plan is shared with their Golden Scholar peer mentor;
- Golden Scholars and their mentor review the plan and seek to develop the student's strengths and goals through participation in clubs/organizations, activities, and internships;
- Golden Scholars participate in a facilitated small-group discussion to discuss common struggles with the transition to college midway through the fall semester.

The strengths-based advising process can contribute to establishing the foundation for students to develop and build upon their natural talents through available on-campus resources and opportunities. The structure of the program allows Golden Scholars to reflect and to engage in that process.

Summary

The goal for the Golden Scholars program is to increase retention among first-generation freshmen in the College of Science. In an effort to positively impact retention, the program provides access to opportunities for the participants to develop knowledge about and confidence in their new environment. Both the Golden Scholars and the First in the Pack programs provide a variety of activities intended to identify and develop their strengths and talents at the University. Examples of activities and opportunities include being assigned a Golden Scholar peer mentor, connecting with other first-generation freshmen in the College of Science, and having the opportunity to network with administrative and academic leaders at the University.

References

Carnevale, A. P. (2007). Confessions of an education fundamentalist. In N. Hoff, J. Vargas, A. Venezia, & M. S. Miller (Eds.), *Minding the Gap: Why integrating high school with college makes sense and how to do it* (pp. 15–26). Cambridge, Massachusetts: Harvard Education Press.

Chen, X., & Solder, M. (2013). STEM attrition: college students' paths into and out of STEM fields. Statistical Analysis Report. NCES, IES, U.S. Department of Education. http://nces.ed.gov/pubs2014/2014001rev.pd.

Engle, J., & Tinto, V. (2008). Moving beyond access: College success for low-income, first-generation students. Retrieved from http://files.eric.ed.gov/fulltext/ED504448.pdf

Hicks, T. (2003). First-generation and non-first-generation pre-college students' expectations and perceptions about attending college. *Journal of College Orientation and Transition, 11*(1), 5–17.

Louis, M. C. (2011). Strengths interventions in higher education: The effects of identification versus development approaches on implicit self-theory. *The Journal of Positive Psychology, 6*(3), 204–215.

National Center for Education Statistics. (2011). Institutional retention and graduation rates for undergraduate students. Retrieved from http://nces.ed.gov/programs/coe/pdf/coe_cva.pdf

Nutt, Charlie L. (2003). Academic advising and student retention and persistence. Retrieved from http://www.nacada.ksu.edu/tabid/3318/articleType/ArticleView/articleId/636/article.aspx

Petty, T. (2014). Motivating first-generation students to academic success and college completion. *College Student Journal, 48*(2), 257–264. Retrieved from http://unr.idm.oclc.org/login?url=http://search.proquest.com.unr.idm.oclc.org/docview/1552786194?accountid=452.

President's Council of Advisors on Science and Technology. (2012). Engage to excel: Producing one million additional college graduates with degrees in science, technology, engineering, and mathematics. PCAST, Washington, DC. Sax, L. J. (2003). Our incoming students: What are they like? *About Campus,* (August), 15–20.

Schreiner, L.A., & Anderson, E. (2005). Strengths-based advising: A new lens for higher education. *NACADA Journal, 25*(2), 20–29.

Soria, K. M. & Stubblefield, R. (2014). First-year collge students' strengths awareness: Building a foundation for student engagement and academic excellent. *Journal of the First-Year Experience & Students in Transition, 26*(2), 69–88.

Talbert, P. Y. (2012). Strategies to increase enrollment, retention, and graduation rates. *Journal of Developmental Education, 36*(1), 22–36.Upcraft, M. L., Gardner, J. N., & Barefoot, B. O. (2005). Introduction. In Upcraft, M. L., Gardner, J. N., & Barefoot, B. O. (Eds.), *Challenging and supporting the first-year student* (pp. 1–14). San Francisco, CA: Jossey-Bass.

Tinto, V. (2006). Research and practice of student retention: What next? *Journal of College Student Retention, 8*(1), 1–19.

Xu, Y. J. (2015) Attention to retention: Exploring and addressing the needs of college students in STEM majors. *Journal of Education and Training Studies, 4*(2), 67–76.

CHAPTER 14

Access to Quality Education

First-Generation Students Reach for College Honors Education

TAMARA M. VALENTINE, PH.D.

Tamara Valentine is the director of the Honors Program at the University of Nevada, Reno. She earned her Ph.D. in linguistics from the University of Illinois, Urbana-Champaign. A sociolinguist, Valentine has published articles and presented papers on topics related to English as an international language, South Asian languages and linguistics, language and gender, and cross-cultural communication. She has taught and conducted research in South Asia, Southeast Asia, and Eastern Europe.

The Value of an Honors Education

Committed to offering an enriched educational experience to all high-achieving students—first-generation, nontraditional, underserved and traditionally advantaged populations—an honors education integrates teaching and learning with research and community engagement to improve the quality of academic achievement and experiential opportunity for all levels of students at a university. Honors programs give dedicated and motivated students the opportunities to demonstrate their knowledge, competence, and interest in different subject areas, to acquire new abilities by becoming a part of an active learning network, and to engage in innovative and different life experiences. College student participation in honors programs leads to greater gains in learning and personal development, higher retention rates, and higher graduate rates. Honors students are more satisfied with their college experience, and better prepared to undertake graduate-level work and gainful employment in their fields.

Although an honors education is attractive to the academically gifted, and open to all high-achieving students, not all eligible college students partake in meaningful academic opportunities and engaged learning practices (Brost & Payne, 2011). Of concern is that first-generation college students, African American students, and transfer students in general underperform in college. Underrepresented student populations are less likely to engage in high-level meaningful learning activities such as an honors education. In general, this group is less likely to apply to honors programs, accept membership, and complete the honors course of study. In addition, first-generation students are less likely to accept an invitation from an honors program, apply on time, and complete an honors curriculum (German & Micomonoco, 2017). To counter this phenomenon, George Kuh (2008) and others recommend that underserved students would greatly benefit from high-impact learning practices (HIPs). Research shows that early participation in engaged educational activities encourages deep learning, promotes more positive student-learning outcomes, raises grade point averages, improves retention rates, and leads to progress toward graduation (Brost & Payne, 2011). Key elements to powerful learning experiences are those that are collaborative, interactive, innovative, engaged, and integrative, especially when students take part in these activities at the start of their academic life (Pascarella & Terenzini, 2005).

While barbs have been thrown at honors education as an elite, privileged system, offering an honors experience is a high-impact practice that benefits all students at an institution. Above all, honors programs expand access to underserved populations of academically talented students. Although research shows that first-generation students do not make the choice to participate in specialized activities such as honors programs, nor engage in high-impact educational practices, the Honors Program at the University of Nevada, Reno finds its membership to be primarily composed of first-generation college students. The Honors Program provides engaging learning practices such as a required first-year seminar, common intellectual and social experiences, an honors residential-living learning community, writing-intensive courses, collaborative assignments, undergraduate research, faculty-student partnerships, global learning, civic engagement, internships, and a senior thesis requirement. The Honors Program at the University of Nevada, Reno has seen a booming number of first-generation

students winning nationally competitive scholarship awards, participating in original research projects and creative activities, interacting
and collaborating with faculty researchers, undertaking international
study, graduating with the completion of a senior thesis, and applying
to top graduate programs. The University's past three winners of the
Truman Scholarship have been first-generation, nontraditional, and/or
Hispanic honors students. Many of its Goldwater scholars are also first-
generation students of color in the Honors Program and underserved
honors graduates are now earning their Ph.D.s at Stanford, Rockefeller,
and Columbia Universities. The Honors Program at the University of
Nevada, Reno makes a difference in the educational lives of underserved students and contributes to their academic and professional
success. As Kuh (2008) suggests, high-impact educational practices
benefit students from diverse socioeconomic and ethnic backgrounds,
and participation in high-impact opportunities such as honors programs leads to gains in retention and persistence to graduation. The
American Association of Colleges and Universities, too, in its Greater
Expectations Initiative supports the effectiveness of high-impact educational practices (2002).

History of the Honors Program at the University of Nevada, Reno

The University of Nevada, Reno pioneered the concept of honors education in the state as early as 1962 and launched its Honors Program
in 1989. It grew to 500 members in 2010, and has graduated over 1,000
students since 1992. The Honors Program attracts more and better
students from across the nation from a wider range of disciplines and
retains highly qualified students (National Merit Scholars, National
Hispanic Scholars, and International Baccalaureates) in the program
at a higher rate than that at the University.

To meet the needs of such students, the Honors Program fosters educational opportunities and student learning gains through a rigorous
academic curriculum, international education, undergraduate research
and creative projects, experiential involvement, and fellowship opportunities. Moreover, the Honors Program builds a learning community
and culture across the campus and student body that shares the mission and vision of excellence in learning and intellectually enriched

opportunities, enhancing student achievement through residential living, global learning, high-level research opportunities, and intellectual leadership to exceptionally able students.

Honors Education and the Superior Student

What began as an enhanced education for the "superior" student, the notion of an honors education at the college level can be traced to such predecessors as the Oxford University tutorial system in the sixteenth century. Personal tutors guided students in proper manners and financial accounting. The tutor was elevated to academic advisor, who critically challenged individual students intellectually and socially at weekly instruction. The foundation of an Oxford education, these one-on-one tutorials in lieu of classes and credit, emphasized inquiry and analysis, independent learning and challenging discussion. A bachelor of arts degree was earned by passing two examinations with a pass or with honors. The comprehensive final exams "were offered as a means for superior students to separate themselves from the rest of their classmates" (Mallet, 1927, p. 168).

In the late nineteenth century, efforts were made to transfer the concept of honors to colleges in the United States. Attempts to replicate the Oxford tutorial method, individualized study, the preceptorial system, and comprehensive examinations were first made by Harvard University, the University of Michigan, Princeton University, and Columbia University. But not until 1922 at Swarthmore College in Pennsylvania did Rhodes Scholar and University president Frank Aydelotte establish the first honors program in the United States and implement the philosophies of active learning, the tutorial system, and the pass/honors approach to other institutions of higher learning (Rinn, 2006, p.72), elements still very much a part of the Swarthmore College Honors Program today. It was only natural for other honors programs to take root across the country.

In 1928, Joseph Cohen helped to establish the Honors Council and later in 1957 the Inter-University Committee on the Superior Student (ICSS). Cohen (1966) devoted his life to "the superior student in American higher education," advocating for the superiority of high-ability students and advancing the notion that the academically talented students must be provided differential learning to meet the intellectual challenges and receive the maximum benefits of the educational system (Andrews, 2011; Rinn, 2003).

In response to the Soviet Union's launch of Sputnik in 1957, the first satellite to orbit the earth, the United States enacted educational reforms infusing billions of federal dollars into its education system. Answering the call for reform, millions of dollars were earmarked primarily for the study of science and engineering in higher education (Douglass, 1999). Universities saw an unprecedented increase in college enrollment; public schools turned their focus on gifted students, handpicking the talented children for upper-level courses; and schools received matching funds for math, science, and foreign languages. Moreover, the notion of the "superior student" was echoed by such academic efforts as the National Merit Scholarship Program (1955) and the College Board Advanced Placement Program (1955) alongside other foundation agencies to accelerate and advance the superior student. By the 1960s, universities across the United States responded to the public's concern that the quality of education in the United States could not stand up to the future technological and scientific advances. In tandem with these efforts, between 1950 and 1963, 232 colleges and universities established new honors programs with special curriculums and programs of studies emphasizing scholastics to meet the special needs and abilities of the academically talented students (Chaszar, 2008, p. 158).

The University of Nevada, Reno, too, a few years later in 1962, in its efforts to attract and retain the "superior" student and reclaim quality education, joined the conversation by establishing the honors study program to promote rigorous academic standards. According to the University's General Catalog, the program offered "talented students' additional opportunity for developing their skills and training their powers of observation, thought, and expression. Successful participation in the program gives superior students the personal satisfaction of having met and mastered the most innovative and challenging program the University offers. In accomplishing this, students enjoy a close relationship with their teachers and fellow honors students" (1988–1989).

As a result of the rapid expansion of honors programs across the country, the National Collegiate Honors Council (NCHC) was formed in 1966. This professional organization had a mission was "to support and enhance the community of educational institutions, professionals, and students who participate in collegiate honors education" (National Collegiate Honors Council, n.d.). And from the early years of "honors," a set of basic characteristics for a fully developed honors program developed to build programs and colleges best suited for the highly capable student population. Institutionalizing set standards and good practices offered honors programs across the nation a no-one-size-fits-all model that could be tailored to fit the mission of each university and its student population. Quality honors programs like the Honors Program at the University of Nevada, Reno were crafted that nurtured intellectual skill, engaged its students in personal and social responsibility, and encouraged applied learning to new complex problems particular to their student populations. The Honors Program at the University of Nevada, Reno and its members are now a part of the national honors community.

Arising as a comprehensive and challenging learning system in the sixteenth century, the collegiate tradition of providing individualized study and open dialogue was "reinvented" as the "superior" student in American higher education—and honors education grew out of this method of learning. Today, more than 1,500 institutions present campus-wide honors education in the forms of honors programs and honors colleges throughout the nation.

Perceived as an education of privilege, pedigree, and promise, honors programs are often viewed as an elite enterprise, accessible to students who are already favored. Advocates for a differentiated honors system of learning submit that, like student athletes and academically underprepared students, the high-ability students, too, should be provided with impactful educational practices and a conducive learning environment to foster their intellectual prowess and receive the maximum benefits of the educational system. However, the image persists that honors programs are fairly homogeneous especially in predominantly white institutions and serve only the advantaged students, who have always profited from intellectually enriched environments, individualized attention, and cognitively engaged activities.

Honors Education and High-Impact Practices (HIPs)

The long history of identifying high-achieving students and nurturing their talents led to the twenty-first century philosophy of engaging honors students in high-impact practices (HIPs) to help retain and ensure the academic success of such students in higher education. According to the Association of American Colleges & Universities (AAC&U), HIPs is an approach to "teaching and learning practices [that] have been widely tested and have been shown to be beneficial for college students from many backgrounds, especially historically underserved students, who often do not have equitable access to high-impact learning." Adopted in 1994, the Basic Characteristics of a Fully Developed Honors Program recommends seventeen best practices that should be shared by all honors programs (Appendix A), many of which involve active learning practices to ensure the success of student learning, retention, and engagement. The Honors Program at the University of Nevada, Reno is no exception; it upholds the "best practices" stated in these national standards. First-year seminars, a common curriculum of special courses, learning communities, writing-intensive courses, collaborative assignments and team-based projects, undergraduate research and creative projects, global and multicultural learning, service learning, community-based learning, internships and field experiences, capstone courses and projects (Kuh, 2008, pp. 9–11), and more, are the backbone of the Honors Program at the University of Nevada, Reno. In fact, full participation in HIPs is required of all students who are members of the Honors Program. HIPs are established to contribute to the success of meeting learning outcomes.

Honors Education for All

Although engaging learning practices are attractive to the academically gifted student, and honors programs are open to all honors-able students, a majority of capable college students do not participate in honors programs and engaged learning activities unless mandated by the conditions of scholarships or University programs. Research indicates that transfer and first-generation students are least likely to engage in high-impact practices compared to other underserved populations (Finley, 2011). And underrepresented students—such as first-generation college students and African American students—are far less likely to apply to honors programs, accept membership, and complete the requirements of the honors program (Kuh as cited in Brownell & Swaner, 2009, p. 26). It is not that institutions with campus-wide honors education do not make efforts to recruit qualified first-generation, minority, transfer, or nontraditional students, they do (Rhea & Goodwin, 2013). Research shows that these segments of students do not actively seek out engaged learning nor take full advantage of the opportunities available to them for various reasons, i.e., stress related to financial reasons, family expectations, and grade point averages (Fonseca, 2014). What does the Honors Program at the University of Nevada, Reno do to enhance the learning and personal development of all students?

Success of the Honors Program to Serve the Underserved

To capitalize on the power of learning, every student ought to have multiple engaged learning experiences each year. George Kuh (2008) makes the claim that high-impact practices have a marked effect on the experiences of underserved students, and the honors experience is strong evidence of deep engagement for student success. In general, honors programs have a higher impact than other learning situations due to their commitment to high-quality, high-impact practices whose characteristics include high performance expectations, authentic, complex tasks, meaningful interactions; challenging ways of thinking, real-world applications; and public displays of competence.

The Honors Program at the University of Nevada, Reno is committed to providing such opportunities for honors students to be engaged in all aspects of active learning throughout their four years at the University. To foster a deep approach to learning and understanding, students are actively involved and connected to the learning process. The following high-impact practices facilitate meaningful learning.

Honors First-Year Seminar

All incoming and new students to the Honors Program enroll in the first-year seminar called Explorations in Honors: Global Perspectives, a course that emphasizes research-based activities, optimal communication skills, service learning, civic education, international study, and responsible self-learning. The seminar allows students to set their own expectations and build confidence in their first semester of college. Students complete writing-intensive assignments; interact with other honors students and faculty; understand empathy and compassion through community service engagement; and design an electronic portfolio that documents their first semester performance, achievements, and success and that authenticates in structured reflections their learning experiences, their personal and academic growth, their potential to make a difference, their graduation plans, and their progress toward future goals.

Honors Residential Scholars Community

Since 2005, with the promise of building a community of scholars, the honors living learning program was characterized by meaningful learning, innovative teaching, and the shared goal of intellectual engagement in a residential educational setting. Incoming students to the Honors Program are eligible to participate in a living learning experience; students enroll in a minimum of three honors classes, interact with other students and work with faculty in and outside of the classroom, and participate in a series of social events.

Honors Bonner Leader Program

With a longtime commitment to diversity and inclusivity, service, and civic engagement, in fall 2017, the Honors Program became a part of the Bonner Foundation's Network of colleges and universities that supports the Bonner Foundation's mission "to provide diverse low-income, underrepresented, and first-generation students with the opportunity to attend college, while engaging their talents and educations in building and supporting communities." Each year the Honors Program provides 10–15 incoming first-year honors students with the opportunity to earn a place as a Bonner Leader with a service-based scholarship in exchange for intensive and meaningful service with a local community partner. In return for the financial award, the Bonner Leaders are expected to donate 8–10 hours a week of community service during the school year. Each first-year class of Bonner Leaders enrolls in its own section of the Honors first-year seminar designed to awaken students to service opportunities and create a culture of volunteerism across campus. A four-year student development model, the Honors Bonner Leader Program at the University of Nevada, Reno hopes to achieve "successful enrollment, retention, and graduation of low-income, first-generation, and diverse students."

Common Intellectual and Social Experiences

The Honors Program offers a number of events and activities that combine curricular with cocurricular: first-year honors retreat, the peer mentoring program, annual series of faculty lectures, career panels and roundtables, Honors Ambassadors, nationally competitive fellowship support, the convocation ceremony, the honors alum chapter, and other student leadership opportunities.

Honors Curriculum of Special Courses

Honors students share a core curriculum of advanced and accelerated classes that culminates in a senior thesis. Taught by top faculty, students enroll in special courses and seminars that are writing and reading intensive and place a strong emphasis on critical thinking, collaboration, in-depth study, cooperative learning activities, and intellectual exchanges.

Undergraduate Research

Honors students are exposed to research on campus early in their career; students conduct faculty interviews, attend the *Great Presentations* faculty lecture series, tour research labs and facilities, observe honors seniors engaged in research, and discover the senior thesis process. The Honors Program requires all honors students to complete a one-credit preparatory research course taught by library specialists to learn about data collection and research tools before undertaking a two-semester thesis under the guidance of a faculty researcher on an original research or creative project. The thesis is orally defended and submitted to the Honors Program as a final publishable manuscript.

Global Learning, International Study, and Outreach Programming

From the first day as a member of the Honors Program, students explore global and multicultural issues in the first-year seminar to gain a deeper understanding of what it means to be an informed global citizen. Class time is devoted to channeling their energy to the needs of the local community such as the Reno refugee resettlement project, daily reading of the *New York Times,* and other activities related to current events; the study of internationally competitive fellowships such as the Rhodes, Marshall, and Fulbright scholarships; and international travel and study abroad. More than twenty percent of honors students participate in international study. They earn academic credit for their study abroad activities, share their international experience through blogs and class presentations, and even satisfy the objectives of the senior thesis by conducting research and collecting data in other countries.

Service Learning and Civic Engagement

Experiential education encourages learning in real-world settings and reinforces comprehension with structured reflection activities. The Honors Program is committed to immersing all honors students in academic service learning and civic engagement to build social responsibility, empathy, and leadership skills. Since 2007, the Honors Program has required that all incoming honors students log a minimum of fifteen hours of service to one of numerous local nonprofit organizations, aligning their major academic interests with community service outcomes. The first-year honors class logs more than 2,000 hours of service in its first semester of college.

Faculty Mentors, Student Partners, and Honors Advisors

The Honors Program provides multiple support systems to help students set goals, design a four-year graduation program, clarify career goals and needs, communicate high expectations, identify resources, and promote personal and professional well-being. The success of the student is contingent on mentors, partners, and advisors to validate the diverse population of students and the academic way.

Internships, Field Experience, and Advanced Research

To gain additional experience, build a professional network, and develop résumés, the Honors Program provides students with internship opportunities in their fields of interest, field experience in their majors in preparation for their careers, and advanced research to pursue projects outside their area of study or to continue ongoing investigation under the guidance of a mentor.

Conclusion

The Honors Program at the University of Nevada, Reno attracts outstanding students who might not have otherwise selected the University of Nevada, Reno as their first college choice. Building on the high-impact educational approaches, the Honors Program supports active student engagement by designing educational experiences committed to offering its students "an Ivy League education at a state school price" (Sullivan & Randolph, 1994) and presenting great opportunity for full participation in academic and campus life. As a result, honors students are more likely to graduate within four years, with a high GPA, and with a repertoire of meaningful experiences that will serve them well in the future (Moritz, 2011; Goodman & Pascarella, 2006).

The Honors Program advances the mission of the University by providing high-achieving students with powerful learning opportunities for innovative research, creative activities, challenging academics, experiential learning, and international and outreach programs. In particular, the Honors Program presents its students with challenges to increase cross-cultural understanding, to expand the capacity for meaningful engagement, to develop a deeper understanding of the learning process, and to build a cultural repertoire necessary to survive in today's complex world.

In its fifty-six years of providing an honors education to high-achieving students, the Honors Program is proud to say that it meets the needs of all students. The Honors Program builds a community of scholars and a culture of engaged learning across the campus, a student body that shares the mission and vision of excellence at all levels of learning. Overall, the Honors Program improves the quality of academic learning and opportunity throughout the University and raises the status of the institution.

References

Andrews, L. (2011). The wisdom of our elders: Honors discussion in *The Superior Student*, 1958–65. *Journal of the National Collegiate Honors Council*. 12 (2), 17–46.

Association of American Colleges and Universities. (2002). Greater Expectations Washington, DC: Association of American Colleges and Universities. www.aacu. org/publications/greater-expectations

Bonner Foundation, Corella & Bertram F. (2018). Retrieved from http://www.bonner.org.

Brost, J., & Payne, K. (2011). First-generation issues: Learning outcomes of the dismissal testimonial for academically dismissed students in the arts & sciences. *New Directions for Teaching & Learning, 127,* 69–79. Doi:10.1002/tl.458101

Brownell, Jayne, & Swaner, Lynn. (2009). High impact practices: Applying the learning outcomes literature to the development of successful campus programs. *Peer Review,* 11 (20), 26–30.

Chaszar, J. (2008). The reinvention of honors programs in American higher education, 1955–1965. Ph.D. Diss. Pennsylvania State University.

Cohen, J. (1966). *The superior student in american higher education.* NY: McGraw-Hill.

Douglass, J. A. (1999). The Cold War, technology and the American University. *Research and occasional paper series:* CSHE.2.99

Finley, A. (2011). Assessment of high-impact practices: Using findings to drive change in the compass project. *Peer Review,* 13 (2), 29–33.

Fonseca Cervantes, Bianca. (2014). Participation of first-generation students in high-impact practices at liberal arts colleges. Occidental College, Thesis.

German, Bess, & Mic-monoco, Justin. 2017. First gens in honors: What works and what is next? Presented at the 2017 Honors education at research Universities Conference, Ohio State University, Columbus, OH, May 25, 2017.

Goodman, Kathleen, & Pascarella, Ernest T. (2006). First-year seminars increase persistence and retention: A summary of the evidence from how college affects students. *Peer Review,* 8 (3), 26–28.

Koopmann, A. (2014). A model for first-generation students least likely to engage in high-impact practices: A mixed methods study. Educational Administration: Theses, Dissertations, and Student Research Paper 199.

Kuh, G. D. (2008). High-impact educational practices: What they are, who has access to them, and why they matter. Washington, DC: Association of American Colleges and Universities.

Kuh, G. D., Kinzie, J., Schuh, J. H., Whitt, E. J., & Associates. (2010). *Student success in college: Creating conditions that matter.* San Francisco, CA: Jossey-Bass.

Mallet, C. E. (1927). *A history of the University of Oxford* (Vol. 3). London: Methuen.

Moritz, B. (2011). Can the elitism of honors help students at non-elite schools? *Journal of the National Collegiate Honors Council,* 12 (2), 65–68.

National Collegiate Honors Council (NCHC). (n.d.). Home - National Collegiate Honors Council. Retrieved from https://www.nchchonors.org/.

Pascarella E. T., & Terenzini, P.T. (2005). *A third decade of research.* Vol. 2 of *How college affects students.* San Francisco: Jossey-Bass.

Rhea, D., & Goodwin, K. (2013). High-impact recruiting: A focus group of prospective honors students. *Honors Practice Online Archive Paper* 200, 111–118.

Rinn, A. (2003). Rhodes Scholarships, Frank Aydelotte, and collegiate honors education. *Journal of the National Collegiate Honors Council Online Archive*, 127, 28–40.

Rinn, A. (2006). Major forerunners to honors education at the collegiate level. *Journal of the National Collegiate Honors Council*, 7 (2), 63–84.

Smith, P, & Scott, R. (2016). Demography of honors: Comparing NCHC members and nonmembers. *Journal of the National Collegiate Honors Council*, 17 (2), 83–101.

Spurrier, R. (2008). The newest "basic characteristics" of a fully developed honors program. Honors in Practice. *Online Archive* 66, 191–198.

Sullivan, R, & Randolph, K. (1994). *Ivy league programs at state school prices*. John Wiley and Sons.

University General Course Catalog 1988–1989. University of Nevada. Reno.

CHAPTER 15

Supporting LGBTQIA+ Students

Geoffrey Green, MA

Geoffrey Green (He/Him/His), a graduate of the University of Nevada, Reno, earned an MA in educational leadership. He works as the assistant director of clubs and organizations through the University's student government. Previously, Green served as a financial aid advisor. He is also the faculty advisor for the Queer Student Union and serves as an advocate for equity and inclusion on campus.

Let us start with a scenario. You are at your institution's recruitment event and during a question-and-answer panel, a parent stands up and says, "My student identifies as nonbinary and uses they/them/theirs pronouns. I am nervous for my seventeen-year-old child to leave the safety of our home, which I am sure is similar to most parents in the room. Could you please tell me what your institution is currently doing for students who identify in the way that mine does to help reassure me that they will be taken care of?" Now if you find yourself rereading this question to figure out terminology and/or are concerned you would have trouble answering it, then this chapter can help both you and your institution make sure you are ready for a scenario like the one presented. The diversity of students that higher education institutions are serving is rapidly growing and evolving along with the coexisting surrounding communities. Institutions of higher learning must become equipped with the necessary tools and resources to properly serve all students pursuing a higher education. Many student affinity groups are seeing services provided for them on their college campus, which are usually prompted by some federal requirement or monetary incentive for the institution. With all the progress higher education institutions have shown within the past several years to ensure they are serving the needs of all students, one student population in particular is often left behind. The lesbian, gay, bisexual, transgender, queer/questioning, intersex, asexual, plus (LGBTQIA+) student community has been treading erasure waters for years in the realm of higher education. Throughout this chapter, you will be taught best practices in making sure your campus is inclusively serving the LGBTQIA+ student population. You will also receive recommendations for specific areas around a college campus that play a key role in the overall campus climate.

One of the primary contributors to the absence of this student group on college campuses is the fact that there are little to no self-reporting opportunities to help quantify this student population. You will often see optional demographic criteria in admissions applications, campus surveys, orientation program reviews, course evaluations, housing applications, etc. These demographic criteria will primarily ask for binary gender (male/female) and race. As practitioners in higher education, we all know that if you are going to ask for funding, you need to be able to present numbers and if there are no numbers for a student group for which you want to provide funding, it makes that argument much harder. The quantification of student affinity groups can be very tricky because of safety, sensitivity, and discrimination risks, so it may be easier for institutions to simply ask for the bare minimum of demographic information that is mandated by law. The institution should develop strategic opportunities to collect more evolved demographic data from the students they serve in a nonintrusive manner. This can be done at the conclusion of any campus event through a generic survey or, even better, in every course evaluation. Course evaluations have a high student participation rate and can serve as a very effective means to collect demographic data on your campus's student population. Data collected through course evaluations will not only help gauge your overall student population but also help you navigate specific demographic trends within course offerings. Voluntary disclosure of sexuality and gender identity should always be asked with a fill-in-the-blank component and should have the option of being submitted anonymously. Figuring out who the students whom you are supposed to be serving is a great starting point for your institution. Another aspect of delivering an LGBTQIA+ inclusive campus is enhancing the overall campus climate for students.

Educating the educators should be an ongoing activity throughout a professional's career in higher education. Campus-wide faculty/staff diversity education programs are essential for the development of an inclusive campus climate. The Safe Zone Project is a national online resource group that provides educational materials for professionals who interact with LGTBQIA+ students. Institutions can find anything from third-party resources to full interactive courses on the webpage. The University of Nevada, Reno has developed a Safe Zone Ally program with the help of numerous resources available on The Safe Zone Project's website. This two-hour program is meant to create a safe space for faculty, staff, and student leaders to learn and ask questions about better serving our LGTBQIA+ students. Departments as well as individuals are able to request a time to take part in this program. Individuals who complete the course are designated an ally on the University of Nevada, Reno campus and are given an ally sticker to put in their space. Departments who have about 90 percent of their staff take part in the course will be given a Safe Zone designation that is made public to students on campus. A two-hour course educating individuals on an entire community is not nearly enough time to truly understand the topic but allows the conversation to at least begin. Participants are reminded that they are not experts when they receive the ally designation and that the point of the program is to really let students know that they are willing to listen, learn, make mistakes, and change any problematic behaviors. One of the main topics that the program brings up is that participants become pronoun positive.

Do you remember our scenario earlier? The parent announced that their child uses they, them, theirs pronouns. This is an example of a student who goes by nongendered pronouns. One of the most important things when communicating with students is that pronouns matter and they should never be assumed. Gender and gender expression is often molded based on societal standards so you must understand that not all individuals desire to be defined by those standards. Most individuals are familiar with gender-specific pronouns such as she/her/hers and he/him/his, so the introduction of nongender pronouns can be alarming to some. They/them/

theirs pronouns are only one example of nongender pronouns, but they can be one of the most difficult ones for people to understand because they are more familiar with using those words to describe people in a plural tense rather than an individual in a singular tense. Please keep in mind that when someone asks you to refer to them using they/them/theirs pronouns that it is not a matter of being grammatically correct but really a matter of respect for that individual. Let us practice using they/them/theirs program in a sentence referring to a singular person.

They has amazing taste in music.
I think I will catch a ride with them.
That cute dog is theirs.

Becoming pronoun positive can have a tremendous impact on your campus climate for LGBTQIA+ students. Some easy yet effective ways to show that you and your campus community are pronoun positive are to add pronouns to nametags, add pronouns to your email signature, and use your own pronouns whenever you introduce yourself. Referring to students using the appropriate pronouns are one of the most important and meaningful things you can do to show you are an ally.

An institution that states that they value diversity is an institution that says they value creating well-rounded citizens to push out into the workforce. A diverse student population is essential for giving students from all backgrounds time to fully embrace, interact, and learn from individuals who are different from themselves. Institutions of higher learning have a responsibility to the students they serve in making sure that these character-building relationships are happening during their students' time on campus. One major factor to ensuring that your campus attracts, retains, and supports diversity is to build a successful infrastructure that is committed to serving those diverse groups. Here is a list of key stakeholders in the creation of an LGBTQIA+ inclusive campus and recommendations these stakeholders can implement on your campus.

Student Services

Admissions and Records

Make sure students have control of their preferred name during attendance. The name listed on the attendance rosters can often be a scary unknown for transgender students. To prevent the instructor from potentially outing a transgender student by calling out their legal name during attendance, make sure your students have some sort of control with providing a preferred name that automatically generates on instructors' student rosters.

Financial Aid & Scholarships

Finances are generally a concern for any student attending college. Federal financial aid programs have little to no area for adjustment since the government regulates them. The financial aid and scholarships office on your campus can still contribute to the inclusivity of LGBTQIA+ students by regulating institutional policies and procedure, especially in the area of scholarships. Try to prevent donors from using gender-specific criteria when creating scholarship agreements. Many scholarships will state male and/or female students in the scholarship agreement, which can eliminate nonbinary individuals from consideration. You can also make sure your scholarship application is using inclusive language when asking for gender and/or sexuality.

Recruitment

The recruitment office is the first point of contact for many students and families. An LGBTQIA+ education program such as Safe Zone is critical for all individuals in this department. A great resource for your campus's recruitment office to look into is Campus Pride. Campus Pride is an online resource targeted to the individuals who identify on the LGBTQIA+ spectrum and are looking to attend a college which has proven to be safe and inclusive. Your institution can be added to this website to show your support for this community. Campus Pride also advertises regional college fairs for your institution to attend that specifically targets LGBTQIA+ students. The Campus Pride Index website, campuspridesindex.org, has a list of recruitment-related questions that are asked of institutions when they're being evaluated as an LGBTQIA+ friendly campus.

Counseling Services

It is very important that you have counseling staff who specialize in LGBTQIA+ issues. College can be a place of exploration for many students because it is their first time away from home. Bernadette Hinojos (They, Them, Theirs) who works at the University of Nevada, Reno's Counseling Services Department gave me a list of what the department does to be inclusive of the LGTBQIA+ student population:

- Intake paperwork asks for pronouns and chosen names. Clinicians can change if necessary, and front-desk staff checks our system for chosen names and pronouns before greeting students.
- The whole department participated in the Safe Zone education program.
- Counseling Services offers an LGBTQIA+ support group.
- Two staff clinicians who are queer-identified and specialize in LGBTQIA+ issues also provide letters for gender-affirmation surgery.
- Throughout the year, there is passive programming regarding LGBTQIA+ issues and education in the waiting room.
- Staff and faculty training throughout the year includes LGBTQ+ issues.
- There is a table at LGBTQIA+ community events.
- There is outreach to different departments on LGBTQ+ issues.

Student Health Center

The student health center plays a vital role in making sure LGTBQIA+ students feel comfortable enough to ask about sexual health issues. Here are a few helpful tips to create a LGTBQIA+ inclusive health center:

- Make sure you have health brochures available that are inclusive of LGBTQIA+ related matters.
- Create a lobby space that assures these students that they will not be looked at differently if they ask a doctor about hormones and corrective surgery.

- Make sure all your intake documentation uses inclusive language.
- Train your staff to not assume gender and sexuality with their patients.
- Take part in on-campus outreach programs specifically for the LGTBQIA+ students.
- Provide free testing and sexual health programs.
- Provide various types of condoms that are useful for all sexual partners.

Diversity Center

The institution's diversity center is usually tasked with being the hub for most diversity related efforts on your campus. Make sure that your campus diversity center is not the only place that you see LGBTQIA+ inclusivity taking place. The University of Nevada, Reno's student diversity center is The Center, Every Student, Every Story. Its primary mission is to serve the greater University mission to "reflect and respect the rich ethnic and cultural diversity of the citizens of Nevada in its academic programs, support programs, and in the composition of its faculty, administration, staff, and student body." This office does a great job making sure our LGBTQIA+ students understand that culture does not stop at race and ethnicity and is inclusive of the gender and sexuality spectrum. The Center facilitates our campus-wide Safe Zone education program and consists of staff who also identify with the LGBTQIA+ community. Community involvement is a big part in creating a great campus-community relationship. The Center plays a strong role in making sure our institution is seen at LGBTQIA+ related community events and will advertise such events to the student body.

Library Services

- Keep an LGTBQIA+ archive.
- Make sure all of your staff has gone through an LGBTQIA+ educational program.
- Provide LGBTQIA+ literature.
- Have a staff member who specializes in queer literature.
- Make sure your library is equipped to order books that a student may request and you do not have.

- This is a public space, so make sure your library has all-inclusive restrooms available.

Academics

Curriculum

Academic curriculum reflects what the institution and surrounding community values. By offering academic courses that directly relate to LGTBQIA+ issues, relations, and development, you are creating a safe academic space that allows all students to have the opportunity to learn. A good starting point to enhance your institution's academic curriculum is to determine how many courses already contain LGTBQIA+ content. Once you have a list of class offerings, you can create a campaign to advertise those specific courses as well as expand course listings, as your institution deems necessary. In an ideal situation, your institution should be striving to create a Queer Studies program that will not only help recruit a more diverse student population to your school but also contribute to the overall campus culture. The Campus Pride Index (campusprideindex.org) has a list of questions about academic life that are asked of institutions to answer when being evaluated as an LGBTQIA+ friendly campus.

Academic Faculty

Academic faculty are crucial to an effectively functioning LGTBQIA+ friendly campus. They are the individuals who build close academic relationships with students and help them prepare for success after the completion of their education. It is imperative that all academic faculty are taking part in some type of LGTBQIA+ educational program and incorporating what they learn into their classroom. Faculty should feel comfortable stating their own pronouns in front of the class when introducing themselves to create an inclusive climate for those who find value in pronoun positivity. Students should be able to tell faculty their preferred name and pronouns and feel like the faculty member will respect and understand that. Another factor that relates to serving LGBTQIA+ students is making sure you have faculty members who identify with them. Hiring more diverse faculty is always on the table for many institutions and methods to improve hiring practices are highly sought.

As much as I would like to disclose the ABCs of hiring diverse faculty on your campus, we would enter a very complex topic that would require an entire chapter in itself. We can, however, speak about steps to make your campus a more desirable workplace for LGTBQIA+ faculty applicants. Your campus needs to not only focus on hiring diverse faculty, but also on retaining them. What is your campus currently doing to make sure your culturally valuable diverse faculty members want to stick around and thrive in your campus environment? Transparency of the positive things your institution is doing for LGTBQIA+ faculty is very important in the recruitment process. Make it known to potential hires what you are doing for them and what they can expect while working at your institution. If your campus is putting in the work to provide a great campus climate for diverse facility, then why not advertise it? The University of Nevada, Reno still has many steps to take to create this ideal campus environment for LGTBQIA+ faculty but has recently taken steps in the right direction. Here is a list of things the University of Nevada, Reno is doing specifically for its LGBTQIA+ faculty.

- LGBTQ+ Task Force: "Created by directive from the chief diversity officer, the LGBTQ+ Task Force makes ongoing assessment of attitudes and conditions throughout the University regarding gay, lesbian, bisexual, trans, and queer persons and issues. The LGBTQ+ Task Force also makes recommendations for changes and seeks implementation of these recommendations on issues such as (1) the University-wide environment for gay, lesbian, bisexual, trans, and queer students, staff, and faculty; (2) appropriate supportive services for such students, staff, and faculty; (3) educational programs for the entire University community; (4) other matters affecting the lives of gay, lesbian, bisexual, trans, and queer community members at University of Nevada, Reno; (5) opportunities for working collaboratively and in concert with a variety of affinity groups" (LGBTQ+ Task Force).
- Creation of a voluntary LGTBQIA+ faculty electronic mailing list that allows easy communication among LGBTQIA+ faculty on various issues as well as promoting faculty social events.

- Participation in the community's annual Pride event that has heavy faculty representation.
- A clear openness to allowing faculty who identify as LGBTQIA+ to speak freely and without fear of reprimand.

Student Life

Housing

On-campus housing can be one of the most rewarding experiences in a college student's life. Housing can play one of the most crucial roles in creating an inclusive environment for students who identify with the LGBTQIA+ community. For institutions which provide on-campus housing, new freshman will often be the dominant population and will serve as one of the first campus climate environments for these students. It is imperative that housing departments do not contribute to the erasure of trans and/or gender-nonconforming individuals because that would set the tone of expectation for the rest of campus life. All-inclusive public restrooms within the communal areas of the housing unit are a great way to enhance the inclusive environment for all residents and/or guests. The Campus Pride Index (campusprideindex.org) has a list of housing and residential life questions that are asked of institutions when they're evaluated as an LGBTQIA+ friendly campus.

Clubs and Organizations

Clubs and organizations on a college campus allow students to seek out individuals who have similar interest and/or backgrounds. These organizations serve as support systems for students and can weigh heavily on a campus's retention rate. Your institution should make sure you have at least one recognized LGTBQIA+ organization for your students. The University of Nevada, Reno has four recognized student organizations. These organizations tend to be the driving forces for change on college campuses so if you are trying to make changes regarding LGBTQIA+ related matters on your campus, the best people to ask for help are the students.

Facilities

Restrooms are a requirement for any building you have on your campus. All-inclusive restrooms may not be a requirement yet but should be a priority. Here is a list of items your campus should make sure you are doing to be inclusive to the LGTBQIA+ community as it relates to facilities:

- Have at least one all-inclusive restroom and/or single-stall restroom in every building.
- Create universal signage for restrooms that are not currently restricted by gender. Faculty, staff, and students at the University of Nevada, Reno recently discussed safe and appropriate signs for restrooms that are not currently restricted based on gender. This is an image of the preliminary conversation on where we would like to take our single-user restroom signage in the future.

FIGURE 15.1. Universal Signage for Restrooms

- Create a campus-wide policy that specifies that individuals may use whichever gender-specific restroom with which they most closely identify. Jodi Thomas (She, Her, Hers), a counselor in the University of Nevada, Reno's Counseling Services Department, has made tremendous strides in implementing LGBTQIA+ related polices, practice, education, and services. She has drafted a restroom policy that your institution can use as reference for creating your own.

   The University of Nevada, Reno supports our community members in using the restroom that feels most comfortable for them, without questioning, harassment, or discrimination. Nevada Revised Statute 651.070 says that all persons are entitled to the full and equal enjoyment of the goods, services, facilities, privileges, advantages, and accommodations of any place of public accommodation, without discrimination or segregation on the ground of race, color, religion,

national origin, disability, sexual orientation, sex, gender identity, or
expression (LGBTQIA+ Community).
- A campus map that displays the location of every single-user restroom should be created for public distribution and access.
- Campus recreational facilities should provide gender-inclusive
locker room options.

School Apparel
University apparel is a way for students, staff, families, and community members to show pride for their institution. Having apparel available that not only addresses institutional pride but also LGBTQIA+
community pride will contribute to the overall campus climate. The
University of Nevada, Reno sells Nevada LGBTQIA+ pride T-shirts
in the bookstore year-round to support our LGBTQIA+ community.
A percentage of revenue made on the sale of these specific shirts go directly to the Queer Student Union organization on campus which uses
it to help fund their scholarship program.

Police Services
The safety of students on campus should be a top priority for institutions of
higher learning. Having emergency procedures and resources on campus
should not only be a requirement, but also transparent and aggressively
advertised to students who may need to use its services. The University
of Nevada, Reno Police Services does a tremendous job in being proactive, contributing to safety by being highly visible on campus as well as
providing easily-accessible resources to students. University Police commander Eric James (He, Him, His) described what the department does to
better serve LGBTQIA+ students on campus. The Blue Light System is a
common system that provides strategically placed blue light poles around
campus. Emergency buttons on the pole instantly contacts police services.
This system in some cases may prove to be more convenient than calling
911 and acts as an additional resource for individuals on campus.

Another resource is the mobile application called "SafePack." "The
SafePack app includes links for campus map downloads, emergency
contacts, emergency plans, report a tip, safe ride access and police and
support services. It also includes a personal safety toolbox with a flash-

light, an alarm, personal safety tips and the University's network of emergency 'blue light' phones" (Staff Report, 2017)

Commander James and his team takes campus safety one step further with ongoing educational programs for their staff that allow their officers to enrich their interactions with a diverse student body. Allowing a space and time for all staff working within police services to become further educated on the people they are meant to serve and protect is one of the most important components to affectively promoting an inclusive police department on your institution's campus. His staff also takes part in an annual education course that is specific to the LGTBQIA+ community. "Our LGBTQIA+ course is a three-hour course that is administered through an on-campus program called Nevada Cares (nvcares.com), and allows our team to learn terminology, understand the importance of pronouns, as well as create a safe environment to ask questions." (James) Institutions seeking to enhance the relationship between police services and the LGBTQIA+ student population should make sure officers are educated on who these people are and the issues they face. Interactions with law enforcement are generally a scary situation for people, especially those who come from marginalized groups. The simple comfort of hearing inclusive language from a police officer will only create positive change for your school's police services as well as contribute to effective communication during potentially stressful encounters. The Campus Pride Index (campuspridesindex.org) has a list of campus safety questions that are asked of institutions when they're evaluated as an LGBTQIA+ friendly campus.

Serving LGTBQIA+ students in many cases may look no different from serving any other student. However, appropriate accommodations and resources should be readily available for all students who need them to succeed throughout their college career. As an institution striving to improve LGBTQIA+ student relations, you must first take a step back and identify the triumphs and pitfalls in your current practices and services. A major takeaway from this chapter is the implementation of an LGBTQIA+ education program for your campus that targets faculty and staff. Changing the attitudes toward the LGBTQIA+ community will help make the implementation of new policies that much easier. The information provided in this chapter should be used as a guiding tool to help create a more inclusive campus for your LGTBQIA+ students.

References

Campus Pride Index. (2006). Retrieved October 17, 2017, from https://www.campus-prideindex.org/.

LGBTQIA Community. (n.d.). Retrieved June 12, 2018, from https://www.unr.edu/counseling/our-services/embracing-our-diversity-and-multiculturalism/lgbtqia-community.

LGBTQ Task Force. (n.d.). Retrieved October 17, 2017, from https://www.unr.edu/diversity/committees/lgbtq-task-force.

The Safe Zone Project [The Safe Zone Project]. (n.d.). Retrieved October 17, 2017, from http://thesafezoneproject.com/.

Staff Report. (2017, August 1). University Police test Emergency Alert System on campus Wednesday. Retrieved June 12, 2018, from https://www.unr.edu/nevada-today/news/2017/emergency-alert-system-drill.

University of Nevada, Reno. (n.d.). About us. Retrieved October 17, 2017, from https://www.unr.edu/the-center/about-us.

CHAPTER 16

Student Veterans

Assistive Technologies and Supports

MARY HEID, BS, CPWA

Mary Heid is a lifelong higher education information technology professional currently employed at the University of Nevada, Reno. Heid is passionate about her work, which focuses on the universal design of technology as a means to provide students equitable access to education and opportunities.

Introduction

Chronic Multisymptom Illness (CMI), also known as Gulf War Syndrome, is present in 49.5 percent of returning U.S. service-persons from Iraq and Afghanistan (McAndrew, 2016). CMI is defined as, "one or more chronic symptoms (present for ≥6 months) from at least two of the following categories: fatigue; mood and cognition; and musculoskeletal" (Fukuda, 1998, p. 981). Forty-three percent of Gulf War veterans return with Traumatic Brain Injury (TBI) (Church, 2009). The University of Nevada, Reno (UNR) served 600 student veterans in Spring 2016 and projected a 10 percent increase for Fall 2016 (Stipech, 2016). Students with cognitive disabilities represent the largest percentage of students served by the Disability Resource Center (DRC) at UNR. Two common cognitive impairments of these veterans include memory impairment and brain injury. This chapter discusses those impairments and some of the assistive technologies and supports that are employed at UNR that help to mitigate the effects of these injuries on the learning outcomes of our student veterans.

Memory Impairments

Memory impairments can limit short-term memory-impacting learning and attention (Hays, 2016). The University offers several resources and assistive technologies to support students' learning. The Tutoring

Center and the Writing Center are both located in the new Pennington Student Achievement Center along with the Nevada Military Support Alliance Veterans' & Military Center (VMC) and the DRC. The Tutoring Center offers study techniques that can aid a student with setting goals, time management, study strategies, group study, and peer tutoring. The Writing Center can help students with writing assignments and offers a fully accessible writing tool, WriteLab, to aid in planning, writing, and revising by providing feedback on clarity, logic, concision, and coherence of written work (WriteLab, 2016).

To supplement the text-to-speech features available in a student's computer or mobile device operating system, the DRC offers free access to JAWS and Read and Write software applications. The screen-reading capabilities of both applications help in auditory learning which can improve attention and memory for some learners. Read and Write Gold, a literacy software, is available on all desktop and mobile platforms and has the capability of highlighting text as it reads aloud which provides multiple means of representation, one of the three principles of Universal Design for Learning. The DRC loans its students Livescribe reading pens which allow students to take synchronized notes while recording lecture audio, helping students with attention (Livescribe, 2016). Students can then review these notes and audio repeatedly. The DRC is available to convert inaccessible course materials to accessible formats for students with documented disabilities. A Spring 2017 pilot of accessible online textbooks and course materials provides all students the opportunity to use the auditory learning tools without needing to request alternate formats from the DRC. Students, including those with memory impairment, will have the most success when they can choose from and combine multiple modes of learning, assistive technologies, and support resources.

Traumatic Brain Injury

Students with Traumatic Brain Injury (TBI) share many symptoms with those who have memory impairments and benefit from the supports and technologies described above to aid with concentration and distraction, short-term memory, and learning new information. Additionally, students with TBI may also suffer from difficulty with language, slower thinking, and hearing and vision loss (Church, 2009). UNR is aggressively working to caption or transcribe all video and audio content available on our websites and in course material provided to students. Captions and transcripts aid students by providing searchable text and the ability to replay material repeatedly and at their own pace and volume. Students who have recently acquired vision impairment, such as a result from TBI, may have limited opportunity to get to campus and benefit from increased online learning opportunities. These online learning opportunities also provide students with TBI the advantage of controlling their physical environment to limit distraction. The DRC offers testing environments that are free of distraction and often are able to provide extended time to take exams for those students who require more time to think and process information.

Outlook

The University of Nevada, Reno is making progress in providing support for all of our students with disabilities. We employ the concepts of Universal Design by seeking accessible products and working with vendors to improve their products when they are not accessible. Faculty employ the concepts of Universal Design for Learning in the classroom to provide more opportunities for more students who learn differently. We continue to rely heavily on assistive technologies to help students with disabilities overcome barriers to higher education. Assistive technologies have a long way to go. For example, these technologies would be more beneficial if integrated into the hardware, software, and applications that students already use rather than a separate tool or file that a student needs to purchase or otherwise acquire through the DRC. Veterans returning with CMI and TBI are not likely to have had experience with a disability office in their high school and may not be aware of the products and services available to them at the University. We need to increase our outreach to those students to ensure they are aware of the resources and overcome any stigma of seeking services at the disability office that may be present in student veterans. Our challenge remains to further employ the strategies of Universal Design so individuals with disabilities are able to independently acquire the same information, engage in the same interactions, and enjoy the same services within the same timeframe as individuals without disabilities, with substantially equivalent ease of use (Accessibility & Technology. University of Nevada, Reno, 2015).

References

Accessibility & Technology. University of Nevada, Reno. (2015). Retrieved November 13, 2016, from unr.edu/accessibility.

Church, T. E. (2009). Returning veterans on campus with war related injuries and the long road back home. *Veterans with Disabilites, special issue of Journal of Postsecondary Education and Disabilities, 22*(1), 43–52. Retrieved November 12, 2016, from https://www.ahead.org/uploads/docs/jped/journals/JPED%20 22_1%20Complete%20Issue.pdf.

Disability Resource Center. University of Nevada, Reno. (2016). Retrieved November 12, 2016, from University of Nevada, Reno: unr.edu/drc.

Fukuda, K. R. (1998). Chronic multisymptom illness affecting Air Force veterans of the Gulf War. *Journal of the American ?Medical Association, 280*(11), 981–988. Retrieved November 12, 2016, from jamanetwork.com/journals/jama/fullarticle/187978.

Hays, K. T. (2016, October). Understanding disability and assistive technology. Division of Disability Resources and Educational Services (DRES). University of Illinois at Urbana-Champaign. Retrieved November 12, 2016, from https://compass2g.illinois.edu/webapps/blackboard/execute/modulepage/view?course_id=_28173_1&cmp_tab_id=_67143_1&mode=view.

Livescribe. (2016). Retrieved November 12, 2016, from livescribe.com/en-us/.

McAndrew, L. M. (n.d.). Iraq and Afghanistan veterans report symptoms consistent with chronic multisymptom illness one year after deployment. *Journal of Rehabilitation Research & Development, 53*(1), 59+. Retrieved from go.galegroup.com/ps/i.do?p=HRCA&sw=w&u=reno&v=2.1&id=GALE%7CA449109155&it=r&asid=92153cdf46dbffe454383d666f570035.

Stipech, D. (2016, May 26). Reflecting on a record year aat the University of Nevada, Reno. *Beyond the Headlines from KUNR.* Retrieved from http://kunr.org/post/reflecting-record-year-university-nevada-reno-0#stream/.

Tutoring Center. University of Nevada, Reno. (2016). Retrieved November 12, 2016, from unr.edu/tutoring-center.

WriteLab. (2016). Retrieved November 12, 2016, from home.writelab.com.

Writing Center. University of Nevada, Reno. (2016). Retrieved November 12, 2016, from unr.edu/writing-center.

CHAPTER 17

Student Conduct

We Are Not the Principal's Office

KIMBERLY THOMAS, JD, LISA MALETSKY, MPH,
and JENNIFER LOWMAN, PH.D.

Kimberly Thomas serves as the dean of students at the University of Nevada, Reno. Thomas, a scholarly practitioner, brought her passion for building networks for students that are healthy, safe, and student success-driven. She shares her passions and insights regularly in her blog, Sister-In-The-Shadow.

Lisa Maletsky, MPH, is the coordinator of student persistence research and doctoral candidate in interdisciplinary social psychology at the University of Nevada, Reno. As an expert in survey methods and statistics, she conducts program assessments and original research for the improvement of programs and services on campus.

Jennifer Lowman, Ph.D., is the director of student persistence research at the University of Nevada, Reno. Her research background is in the social psychology of educational and occupational pathways. She supports program assessment and conducts original research for the continual improvement of programs and services on campus.

The activities of the Office of Student Conduct (OSC) and its mission are often misunderstood. Many believe the OSC focuses on only punitive sanctioning of students who violate University policies. In essence, we are seen as the stereotypical "principal's office." where students go to be punished. This reductionist view fails to account for the myriad of ways the OSC reintegrates students with challenges into the campus community. The OSC works from the premise that integration in the campus community is key for students' success in college (Astin, 1984; Pascarella & Terenzini, 2005; Tinto, 1993). For first-generation students this is of particular importance because research tells us that these students are less likely to feel a sense of belonging on campus, they face greater difficulty participating in extracurricular activities, and they are less likely to engage with on-campus peers (Edman & Brazil, 2009; Padgett, Johnson, and Pascarella, 2012; Pascarella, Pierson, Wolniak, and Terenzini, 2004). Additionally, these students face unique stress that stems from navigating college bureaucracies without family support, as well as feeling they are the lone representatives of their communities (Daniel Valle, personal communication, June 26, 2017). In 2016, 21 percent of students served by the OSC were first-generation students; the vast majority of these first-generation students were also from low-income households (92 percent).

Students often enter the OSC in need of mentorship. Approaching these students with flexibility and open-mindedness is key. We play the role of mentor and facilitator to guide students as they navigate expectations and acclimate to college cultural norms. Students can expect that the OSC staff will work with them to develop an individual educational life plan tailored to help them manage their particular issues and challenges. This is done by redirecting the attention of students to focus on their educational and career aligned goals. By focusing on end goals, productive discussions can be had about making thoughtful choices, the potential consequences of those choices, and the benefits of collaborations in our learning community. Improving students' perceptions of social support and encouraging campus integration have been linked to academic success, including improved persistence and grades (Edman & Brazil, 2009). Thus, the OSC staff provides prevention education *and* helps students refocus on their educational goals.

The impact of this approach is best exemplified in a recent interaction with two first-generation college students who enrolled in a long-term OSC sobriety program. These students reported that for the first time on campus they believed the staff cared about them, listened to them, and wanted to help them be successful in school and in life. The OSC staff were able to turn a potentially negative experience of being summoned to the "principal's office" into an opportunity to enhance students' efficacy, motivation to succeed, and perception that our campus cares about their success.

In the OSC, there is an expectation that students who visit have problems and a unique story. We directly communicate that we are not going to judge the student or expect perfection—we are not the principal's office. Unlike in the academic disciplines, we do not grade them, they are not expected to get an "A." We assure students that we want them to succeed and thereby negate stereotypes and decrease performance anxiety. After spending time with a classroom of NevadaFit students, one student commented that the OSC is "a place where no judgment is guaranteed and a place to talk to someone."

Taking time to listen to a student in crisis often helps to reveal an underlying issue and barrier to student success. For instance, a student was referred to the OSC for sending a "threatening email" in which the student expressed anger about being asked to leave on-campus housing (a regular occurrence after a student's freshman year). After listening to the student, we discovered that the student was fearful about finding a new place to live and paying for off-campus rent. What was perceived as a threatening email was really a plea from a desperate student with no safety net, a student without the same level of family resources as her peers from middle- and upper-class backgrounds. First-generation students are generally under more financial strain during their time in college and do not have the same economic safety nets of their traditional peers (Conley & Hamlin, 2009). As such, we introduce students to the safety net that the Division of Student Services provides. In this case, we connected the student to Residential Life for support searching for off-campus housing and to the Financial Aid office for assistance to pay her rent. No punitive sanction was required.

Much of what the OSC does is connect students to on-campus resources. The OSC office regularly interacts with the Equal Opportunity and Title IX Office, the Career Studio, New Student Initiatives, the ASUN Center for Student Engagement, the Provost's Office, Residential Life, Counseling Services, the Disability Resource Center, the Joe Crowley Student Union, the Wolf Shop, Health Services, the Tutoring Center, and Facilities Services. This list does not include every opportunity presented for collaboration, but it does demonstrate that the OSC can be a central point of integration for students with challenges.

Transitioning students from the OSC office to another on-campus resource occurs in a personal manner, either through a phone call or walking the student to the particular office. This type of personal approach resembles the care taken by a track athlete handing off a baton in a relay race. The relay team (our campus community) must take excellent care of the baton (the student) on the race to the desired end (graduation in four years or less). We regularly hear from students that the OSC was "a gateway to all resources." The OSC staff encourages students to expand their circles of support to promote choices that result in academic and career successes.

We have learned that students from underrepresented backgrounds often need the recognition that their challenges are normal, and validation that their questions and doubts are common. First-generation students worry that their concerns may be misunderstood or dismissed as "dumb." They often find themselves second-guessing their ability to "fit in" based on widely accepted stereotypes about not being "college material" or college-ready (Banks-Santilli, 2014; McKay & Devlin, 2016). Stereotypes such as these can cause students to underperform (Steele, 2010), especially in situations where performance really matters to the student or to their family and friends.

First-generation students have confided in the staff that they are concerned about disappointing their families and not being good role models for their siblings. This is also why a nonjudgmental approach is crucial for connecting with students. Many of the pressures students face are not related to academic or social integration on campus, but instead to families and friends at or back home. Essentially, students need someone guiding them through the process of connecting with campus professionals who can teach them to speak the language of higher education and yet maintain their connection with home. We validate their problems, provide opportunities to access resources, and expand their circles of support to make choices that result in academic and career successes.

We know our office has had an impact through the comments students and departmental staff share. The ultimate compliment paid to the OSC was when a student characterized us as "*Hellacool!*" He did not like having to complete the terms of his sanction, but enjoyed his association with the staff in the office. Many students have returned over the years to share with the OSC how we helped them turn their lives around when they were at their lowest point. Students enter the OSC office at a critical juncture in their lives, and although the majority of our students do not rave about contact with the OSC, we know that our efforts establish foundations for student success. In addition to the hugs and high fives, our quantitative assessments also show that students come to appreciate their time with us. For instance, we ask students to rate their overall experience against their initial expectation when they first came to OSC and have found that students' ratings *increase* on average three points from a negative expectation to positive outcome after they complete their educational program.

Going forward we are going to make an effort to document service referrals and identify resource use before and after contact with the OSC. Tracking referrals will help map each student's resource network and understand our impact on building the community students need to get to graduation. While many on campus see the student's success from the standpoint of test scores and grades, the OSC recognizes that the conduct and choices students make socially also impact their learning outcomes and academic achievement. We support the integration of all students, especially those who need validation they earned the right to be here. The staff wants the students to "believe they [can] be successful" (Rendon, 1994). The Office of Student Conduct exists to support students and all other departments concerned with the retention and persistence of first-generation and underrepresented students on our campus. Send them our way. We are not the principal's office. We are here to help.

References

Astin, A. W. (1984). Student involvement: A developmental theory for higher education. *Journal of College Student Personnel, 25,* 297–308.

Banks-Santilli, L. (2014). First-generation college students and their pursuit of the American dream. *Journal of Case Studies in Education,* 5, 1–32.

Conley, P. A. & Hamlin, M. D. (2009). Justice-learning: Exploring the efficacy with low-income, first-generation college students. *Michigan Journal of Community Service Learning,* 16(1),47–58.

Edman, J. L., & Brazil, B. (2009). Perceptions of campus climate, academic efficacy and academic success among community college students: An ethnic comparison. *Social Psychology of Education,* 12(3), 372.

McKay, J. & Devlin, M. (2016) 'Low income doesn't mean stupid and destined for failure': challenging the deficit discourse around students from low SES backgrounds in higher education. *International Journal of Inclusive Education*, 20:4, 347–363, DOI: 10.1080/13603116.2015.1079273

Padgett, R. D., Johnson, M. P., Pascarella E. T. (2012). First-generation undergraduate students and the impacts of the first year of college: *Additional Evidence*, 244.

Pascarella, E. T., Pierson, C. T., Wolniak, G. C., and Terenzini, P. T. (2004). First-generation college students: Additional evidence on college experiences and outcomes. *Journal of Higher Education*, 75, 249–284.

Pascarella, E. T., and Terenzini, P. T. (2005). How college affects students: a third decade of research (2nd ed.). San Francisco: Jossey-Bass.

Rendon, L (1994). Validating culturally diverse students: toward a new model of learning and student development. *Innovative Higher Education* 19(1) 40.

Steele, C. (2010). Whistling Vivaldi: How stereotypes affect us and what we can do. Norton & Company, Inc., New York.

Terenzini, P. T., Rendon, L. I., Upcraft, M. L., Millar, S. B., Allison, K. W., and Gregg, P. L. et al., (1994). The transition to college: Diverse students, diverse stories. *Research in Higher Education*, 35, 57–73.

Tinto, V. (1993). Leaving college: rethinking the causes and cures of student attrition (2nd ed.). Chicago: University of Chicago Press.

Valle, D. M., personal communication June 26, 2017. Social capital and low-income, first-generation latino male college students.

CHAPTER 18

Four First-Generation Student Experiences

Gemma's Story

Gemma Beltran, BS, BA, (2017)

Gemma Beltran is a Filipino American who is known for her passion for philanthropic initiatives. During her college years, she was also involved with the TRiO Scholars Program, Dean's Future Scholars Program, Honors Program, Nevada First, and Kappa Phi Lambda Sorority. Beltran currently holds two degrees: a bachelor of science in biology and a bachelor of liberal arts in spanish with a minor in analytical chemistry.

Taking initiative is the most important first step to be an "entrepreneur" in creating undergraduate experiences. Doing so, however, requires the willingness to step out of your comfort zone to ask questions and to ask for help.

This is something I learned the summer before I attended college when I wanted to collect school supplies for students who attended the elementary schools I attended in Reno and in the Philippines. I reached out to the director of the University of Nevada, Reno's student government, who was my supervisor at that time, to ask for help with the fundraiser. With her help and that of individuals throughout the community, I collected more than 1,800 school supplies, which I distributed to Libby C. Booth and Saludares-Cali Elementary School.

This would not have been possible without the community's assistance. However, if I didn't ask for help, I would not have made the connections that I obtained and I would not have been as successful with the fundraiser as I was. This life success shows that in order to be successful, you must continually ask questions and ask for assistance. You want to do something but don't know how to be suc-cessful? Ask people who are already successful with it. You want to be involved but do not know where to start? Ask people who are already involved. Individuals in higher education are there to grow and help other people. Therefore, do not be afraid to ask questions. That is the only way that you can start to create an unforgettable experience at the University.

To create your own opportunities at the University of Nevada, Reno, you must also take action. Nothing in life is free. You must work for it. Therefore, to have those opportunities, work to have them. Ask yourself: "What have I always wanted to try?" "How can I leave a mark in the world?" and "What makes me happy?" Once you answer those questions, ask yourself, "What am I doing to fulfill those?" Take it upon yourself to take action at that moment. Do not wait a few days or weeks to take action because eventually those days will add up to weeks, then months, and then years. It will then add up to the point where you will say, "I wish I would have done that." This is your chance to make your dreams a reality. You want to do something? Do it right then and there. Sometimes the longer you wait, the more time you will have to talk yourself out of it.

During my sophomore and junior year of college, I was recom-mended to apply for the GEAR UP Alumni Leadership Academy to be an alumni leader and for the General Undergraduate Research Award to work on a research project. Upon hearing about the opportunities, I was ecstatic but also worried because I wasn't sure if I would be able to get them. Despite this fear, I decided to just do it and fill out the applications. After a few weeks of submitting them, I was informed that I received both the position and the award. If I would not have taken the action, I would not have been given the opportunity to go to Washington, D.C.-to talk to Nevada politicians about GEAR UP, and I would not have been able to work on a research project that was fully funded for a year. To create your own opportunities, you must have the courage to take risks and action. Those efforts will later create even more opportunities for you in the future.

Liliana's Story

Liliana Davalos, MPH (2015, 2017)

Liliana Davalos is a native Nevadan and a first-generation college student. She attended the University of Nevada, Reno, where she received a bachelor's degree in biology in 2015 and a master's of public health in 2017. Davalos currently works for Immunize Nevada, a nonprofit organization in Reno.

As a first-generation student, I benefited from being involved with various organizations. Since I lived on campus, I did not have to commute, thus allowing me to become involved with student clubs and organizations. One of my first leadership roles was serving as a resident assistant. This opportunity challenged me to step outside my comfort levels and speak publicly to student audiences. It also provided a platform to interact with diverse students and develop a residential community.

Another opportunity was working for the undergraduate student government as a student event programmer. I was responsible for organizing events, requiring me to collaborate with countless students and organizations. This position forced me to communicate with University faculty as well as Reno leaders, which facilitated a connection with the local community.

Finally, I was also involved with the Nevada Student Ambassadors, where I served as a student recruiter and conducted campus tours for prospective families. As an ambassador, I strengthened my appreciation for my University, and it is through this organization that I met my closest friends. These opportunities gave me perspective about the true value of my higher education. I received invaluable support from my peers, and I gained strong mentors who reinforced the importance of completing my bachelor's degree.

If I had not taken advantage of these opportunities, I would have felt alone on a big campus and I would not have been prepared to achieve my professional goals. These experiences outside of the classroom were complementary to the academic curriculum, contributed to my personal development, and are the highlight of my collegiate experience.

Maria's Story

Maria Lee-Camargo, EdM (2015)

Maria Lee-Camargo is working as a first-grade teacher in the Clark County School District. She completed a bachelor of arts in psychology from the University of Nevada, Reno and then pursued a master's of education in early childhood education from the University of Nevada, Las Vegas.

During my four years at the University of Nevada, Reno, I was fortunate to be a part of the Residence Hall Association (RHA), worked as a community assistant (CA) in Canada Hall, and worked as a research assistant (RA) for the Psychology Department and the Human Development and Family Studies program. I started my freshman year by focusing on my academics and got involved in RHA during my second semester. Since then my life changed drastically, and I found myself wanting to more involved and more challenged.

As part of the RHA I was able to work as events director, where I worked with other students to create events that would bring our residents together to make memories. This job gave me the chance to learn about my own leadership and organizational skills in a fun and creative way. As a CA I was able to create meaningful relationships with my residents in an effort to make their time at the University safe, engaging, and worthwhile. Through programming and day-to-day interactions, we created our own unique community within a larger environment. It was an experience that challenged me on a professional and personal level on a daily basis. Working as an RA gave me the chance to explore my academic goals through hands-on experience. This experience helped me make connections and created opportunities for me to engage with families and students to learn about what I could do to make an impact on their daily lives.

Getting involved on campus both socially and academically took me out of my comfort zone and challenged my skills and abilities. Had I not experienced this involvement I would not have enjoyed my time at the University as much. Most of my memories and friendships stemmed from my involvement in these positions. Participating helped me overcome personal challenges and reassured me that I was a valuable part of the University community. My time and experiences at the University impacted my academics, relationships, skills, and perspectives, and made it that much harder for me to leave. I cultivated friendships and memories that I would not change for anything, and that I know will last me for years to come.

Ivón's Story:

Ivón Padilla-Rodríguez, BA in History, BA in Philosophy (2015)

Ivón Padilla-Rodríguez is a doctoral student in Columbia University's Department of History. She graduated from the University of Nevada, Reno in 2015 with degrees in history and the philosophy of ethics, law, and politics. She is the co-editor of the award-winning *The Country I Call Home* and a Truman Scholar.

For low-income, first-generation high school graduates, choosing to enroll in an institution of higher education is among the most important decisions they will make in their lifetime. It is telling that less than 11 percent of low-income, first-generation students will have earned a bachelor's degree within six years of enrolling in postsecondary education, according to the Pell Institute (2011). It is precisely because first-generation high school students do not have college-educated parents, that those who make it to college and graduate do so by being resourceful and inventive.

I know this to be true from firsthand experience. My parents are immigrants from Guadalajara, Jalisco. In Mexico, they did not finish their high school education. My parents came to the United States to provide our family a better life. Indeed, the life they envisioned for us— the life they would not have been able to secure for us in Mexico—had educational opportunity at its core. Because my parents did not know how to navigate U.S. college admission and financial aid processes, I applied to colleges and scholarships with little support. I was a student at an underprivileged, Title I high school in North Las Vegas, and my teachers and counselors were limited by their enormous caseloads to provide a student like me with the support I needed.

Although I incessantly searched for scholarship opportunities as a high school senior and graduated as class valedictorian, I was awarded only a small percentage of the awards to which I applied. In my experience, this is a usual outcome for students with little knowledge about expository writing and competitive application strategy. So, I enrolled at the University of Nevada, Reno (UNR) because of its low cost for in-state students. Little did I know, however, that the environment at a public institution such as UNR would become the perfect incubator for the ingenuity I had just begun to develop as a high school senior.

At UNR, I was a member of its Honors Program, where I had access to a vibrant, intellectual community and small classroom sizes. In part, I succeeded at UNR to the extent that I did simply because the Honors Program bombarded me with information about every possible opportunity at my disposal.

Exposure to knowledge and information through mentorship is a critical first step to curating a competitive, world-class undergraduate experience anywhere, especially for underrepresented students. In my first semester of college, the directors of the Honors Program informed me of study abroad, public service, nationally competitive fellowships, and research opportunities.

The close-knit nature of the UNR Honors Program made it possible for me to secure the kind of sustained, one-on-one mentorship that can propel any student, but especially a traditionally disadvantaged student like me, into the national spotlight. Because the Honors Program required me to carry out public service projects in my community and reach out to University professors for interviews about their research, I inevitably formed a network of supportive advisors within and outside of my university.

With the help of mentors on and off campus, I managed to accumulate a list of accomplishments I never before thought possible by the time I graduated with my bachelor's degrees: I earned nearly $200,000 in scholarships and fellowships; I founded an international children's theater program for low-income Latino and immigrant youth; I presented my academic research to members of the United States Congress; I co-published a book and inaugurated a scholarship fund for students with the profits; I established educational initiatives and mentoring programs that served hundreds of at-risk students; and I accepted an admission offer from Columbia University for my Ph.D.

My undergraduate experience was made possible by a multifaceted process that was mutually beneficial for both my institution and myself. This process included securing the support of individual mentors and exposure to opportunity. Surely, the profound impact individual advisors had on me cannot be understated. The insights and knowledge of opportunities possessed by a history professor and the directors of the Honors Program and UNR Latino Research Center undoubtedly shaped my trajectory. But underrepresented students who successfully enroll at college institutions are necessarily very resilient, given the obstacles they face. We make the most of our lack of guidance and resources at home and seek out or create our own opportunities in many cases.

Truth be told, professors around me identified my promise and talent because I was relentless in my pursuit of educational advancement. I spoke to three professors who declined to work with me on independent research projects until the fourth finally agreed to supervise my work. I applied for numerous grants and scholarships, many of which were rejected, before the directors of the UNR Honors Program took notice of me.

The second step to curating a competitive, world-class undergraduate experience is to identify talented students and nurture their intellectual curiosities at all costs. Ensuring they gain access to communities where they will be both supported and challenged, and have the resources necessary to actualize their goals, will yield unprecedented results. As an undergraduate, I discovered a like-minded community in my University's Latino student organization, where I gained exposure to additional opportunities for academic and professional development. Not to mention, I learned about funding opportunities and gained the connections necessary to establish educational initiatives.

I had to constantly campaign for money to fund the initiatives I knew my community needed, however. One way undergraduate institutions can help address this issue and support ambitious students is by allotting a small amount of money for undergraduate project grants. As I met students around the country with whom I won nationally competitive awards, I learned more and more that their institutions unquestionably supported their commitment to public service and helped fund their projects.

In sum, the ingredients necessary for the creation of a competitive undergraduate experience include: identifying talented students; investing in one-on-one mentorship; exposing students to information about opportunities for professional and academic advancement as early as is appropriate; fostering the development of diverse intellectual communities outside of the classroom; and offering resources for students to be entrepreneurial, however small they may be.

First-generation and other traditionally disadvantaged students are naturally very imaginative out of necessity. Undergraduate institutions can ensure that students like me thrive on their college campuses by developing and sustaining interpersonal and financial resources for their students. Simply communicating the availability of on-campus and external opportunities to students can transform an already resilient, underrepresented student's academic and professional trajectory. This process is a rather symbiotic one, for institutions and professors possess the knowledge and resources with which to complement a traditionally disadvantaged student's resoluteness. After developing an infrastructure for underrepresented students to thrive, institutions can then harness the insights of students who have been successful on college campuses by encouraging them to share their insights with new students to continue the cycle of knowledge sharing, mentorship, and social entrepreneurial activity.

References

Pell Institute. (2011, December 14). Pell Institute Fact Sheet. Retrieved from http://www.pellinstitute.org/downloads/fact_sheets-6-Year_DAR_for_Students_Post-Secondary_Institution_121411.pdf.

PART III

Success After Graduation

Support does not end when the student crosses the stage at commencement, nor when their degree is conferred upon them. Students, or alumnus, may seek further education to enhance their ability to find a job in the competitive marketplace. This section highlights two programs at the University of Nevada, Reno: The GradFIT and the Post-Baccalaureate Program at the University of Nevada, Reno School of Medicine, which further prepare those students who want to obtain higher degrees to do so with the support and guidance they need to take those steps on their own.

CHAPTER 19

Beyond the Baccalaureate

McNair Scholars Program

PERRY FITTRER, PH.D.

Perry Fittrer is the assistant director of the McNair Scholars Program at the University of Nevada, Reno. His professional and research interests include academic-help seeking, access and success in graduate education, and undergraduate research. He holds a Ph.D. in education from the University of Nevada, Reno.

As the other authors have noted throughout this book, first-generation, low-income, and underrepresented students face significant challenges with respect to access, opportunity, and success in postsecondary education. Educational access and opportunity beyond the baccalaureate are particularly troubling challenges for this student population. Opportunity for graduate education requires not only access and success at the baccalaureate level but also a transition from the margins of academe to the very center of academic culture, thought, and bureaucracy. For small cohorts of students at the University of Nevada, Reno (UNR) the successful transition to graduate education is facilitated by the McNair Scholars Program.

Beyond the Baccalaureate

Academe has a problem: diversity of academic faculty. This lack of diversity manifests itself in terms of ethnicity and socioeconomic status. According to the National Center for Educational Statistics (2016) more than 75 percent of tenured and tenure-track academic faculty nationwide identify their ethnicity as white. Because of this, first-generation, low-income, and underrepresented students often do not see themselves, their experiences, and their cultures expressed in the classroom or research environments.

To address this lack of diversity, the pipeline of diverse potential faculty members must be developed. However, this pipeline is lagging; 72 percent of doctoral degrees awarded nationwide were earned by white students (NCES Survey of Earned Doctorates, 2016). In terms of socioeconomic status, 69 percent of doctoral degrees nationwide are earned by students whose parents have a bachelor's degree or higher (NCES Survey of Earned Doctorates, 2016). Additionally, students from low-income, first-generation, and diverse backgrounds are clustered in master's degree programs, and non-STEM fields, and take more time from baccalaureate completion to doctoral degree completion (NCES Survey of Earned Doctorates, 2016; Cataldi, Siegel, Shepherd, & Cooney, 2014).

For students at Nevada, graduate education is not at the forefront of their career and educational goals. Only 9 percent of Spring 2016 bachelor's degree recipients reported plans to enroll in graduate school of any type for the following academic year (UNR, Office of Student Persistence Research, 2016). For low-income, first-generation, and underrepresented students, that number was 1 percent

McNair Scholars at Nevada

The McNair Scholars Program at the University of Nevada, Reno plays a small but vital role in addressing the challenges of faculty diversity and the development of a diverse faculty pipeline. The McNair Program is a federally funded TRiO program operated under a five-year, $1.2 million grant from the United States Department of Education and was first awarded to the University of Nevada, Reno in 2002. Although program models vary, 151 institutions across the country operate McNair Programs.

The program at the University of Nevada, Reno serves twenty-seven undergraduates annually with the goal of providing research opportunities and other related academic experiences that promote the acquisition of the doctoral degree (Ph.D.) for first-generation, low-income, and underrepresented juniors and seniors. Two-thirds of program participants must be both low-income and first-generation while the remaining participants may be from a group underrepresented in graduate school, namely: American Indian/Alaskan Native, black or

African-American, Hispanic or Latino, or Native Hawaiian or Pacific Islander. For 2015–2016, 79 percent of participants were both first-generation and low-income.

Program Model

To achieve the goal of preparing students for doctoral study, an intensive and intrusive program model is utilized. The model consists of four primary components: undergraduate research, faculty mentoring, academic and personal coaching, and graduate school preparation.

Undergraduate research with a faculty member is deemed a high-impact and life-changing practice for students (Kuh, 2008). Despite being a research institution, undergraduate research is limited and exclusive at UNR. Only 30 percent of first-generation students reported being involved with undergraduate research, and fewer than 17 percent of underrepresented students participated (UNR NSSE Survey, 2013). However, undergraduate research experiences greatly improve the probability of graduate school enrollment (Hurtado, Eagan, Figueroa, & Hughes, 2014) and are a critical consideration in the admissions process (Posselt, 2016).

The McNair Program requires each student to complete at least one undergraduate research project before graduation. To accomplish this, students are connected with an academic faculty member who guides them through a research project in their desired graduate field of study. Each spring, McNair students enroll in a one-unit course, where they learn research development basics and complete a written research proposal. During the summer, students complete an eight-week research program completing a minimum of 120 hours of research activity with their faculty member. After the summer program, students present their research at a national academic conference and submit a journal-ready publication. The research experience provides students with an immersive experience in their academic discipline, necessary research training for graduate school, as well as exposure to faculty/graduate student life.

Throughout the research experience, the faculty mentoring component of the program is critical. A formal mentoring relationship is established between each student and an academic faculty member upon students' admission to the program. The program facilitates this relationship and provides ongoing training and support for both parties. The faculty mentor not only assists with research but also exposes the student to the inner workings of faculty life, their academic discipline, and the graduate education process. The mentoring relationship is structured in much the same way as it is in graduate school. Thus, the faculty mentor relationship provides the student with the skills needed to establish a productive relationship with their faculty advisor/chair when they enroll in graduate school. The mentor is also invaluable in supporting the student in the program selection and application process for graduate study.

Academic and personal coaching can have a positive impact on student outcomes (Bettinger & Baker, 2011). As such, each McNair staff member serves as a coach for designated students participating in the program. Coaching involves frequent and intrusive programmatic contact with students of no less than once per month. Program staff members monitor academic progress, hold regular individual and group meetings, develop academic and personal goal agreements with benchmarks, and the support the development of noncognitive factors such as self-advocacy and decision making. This coaching is designed to support the students in their academic and personal development through the undergraduate experience so that they may have the skills necessary to be successful in graduate education.

Perhaps most importantly, the McNair Program provides comprehensive graduate school preparation services. Slightly more than 13 percent of all students entering the University of Nevada, Reno plan to pursue a doctoral degree compared to 19.1 percent nationwide (CIRP, 2016). However, plans to enroll in graduate school drop significantly by the time of graduation for UNR students. Only 9 percent of bachelor's degree graduates from UNR plan to enroll in graduate school and 1 percent or less of McNair eligible students intend to go to graduate school. Additionally, the population of students served by the McNair Program often find themselves at the margins of two cultures, that of their family and friends and that of the academic community (Espino, 2014).

Thus, the McNair Program provides services to assist students in being prepared academically and culturally for graduate study. In terms of academics, students learn about research in their field, complete a four-week intensive GRE Exam course, and are supported in their coursework through tutoring. Students are also prepared for graduate school through the development of positive academic skills, mindsets, and behaviors such as time management, goal setting, and self-regulation. Culturally, students explore their own identity as a student and scholar through self-reflection, group discussions, and workshops. This exploration exposes students to the unique culture, norms, language, and traditions of academe while encouraging them to articulate the value of their own identities in contributing to and changing academe for the better.

Outcomes

The McNair Program has been very successful in achieving its goals and has served a total of 157 students since program inception. The most recent four-year graduation rate (2012 first-time, full-time freshman cohort) was 100 percent. The Fall 2016 to Fall 2017 retention rate was also 100 percent with current 2016–2017 participants having an average GPA of 3.67.

Eighty-two percent of participants have enrolled in graduate school with eight of the nine 2017 graduates enrolled in graduate school for the following fall. Eight program alumni have earned Ph.D. degrees, four have earned professional doctorates, and sixty-seven master's degrees have been earned. Additionally, thirty-six alumni are currently enrolled in Ph.D. programs, and fifteen are enrolled in master's programs. Program alumni have attended graduate schools across the country including many top research universities.

Conclusion

First-generation, low-income, and underrepresented students need to pursue graduate study to address the underrepresentation of those populations in postsecondary faculty. Through the intensive program model of the McNair Scholars Program at the University of Nevada, Reno, student participants have been very successful in accessing and succeeding in graduate study.

References

Bettinger, E.P., Baker, R. (2014). The effects of student coaching an evaluation of a randomized experiment in student advising. *Educational Evaluation and Policy Analysis*, 36(1), 3–19.

Cataldi, E.F., Siegel, P., Shepherd, B., & Cooney, J. (2014). Baccalaureate and beyond: A first look at the employment experiences and lives of college graduates, four years on (B&B:08/12) (NCES 2014–141). National Center for Education Statistics, Institute of Education Sciences, U.S. Department of Education. Washington, DC.

Cooperative Institutional Research Program at the Higher Education Research Institute at UCLA. (2016). 2016 CIRP freshman survey institutional profile reports. University of Nevada, Reno.

Espino, M. (2014). Exploring the role of community cultural wealth in graduate school access and persistence for Mexican American Ph.D.s. *American Journal of Education* 120 (4).

Hurtado, S., Eagan, K., Figueroa, T., & Hughes B. (Apr 2014). *Reversing underrepresentation: The impact of undergraduate research programs on enrollment in stem graduate programs.* Los Angeles: Higher Education Research Institute, UCLA

Kuh, G. D. (2008). *High-impact educational practices: What they are, who has access to them, and why they matter.* Washington, DC: Association of American Colleges and Universities.

National Science Foundation, National Center for Science and Engineering Statistics. (2016). Doctorate recipients from U.S. universities: 2015. Special report NSF 17-306. Arlington, VA. Retrieved from www.nsf.gov/statistics/2017/nsf17306/.

National Survey of Student Engagement Survey, (2013). NSSE 2013 high-impact practices University of Nevada, Reno. Retrieved from https://www.unr.edu/assessment/institutional-data.

Posselt, J. R. (2016). *Inside graduate admissions: Merit, diversity, and faculty gatekeeping.* Cambridge, MA: Harvard University Press.

University of Nevada, Reno Office of Student Persistence Research. (2016). *Spring 2016 UNR graduates reporting plans to enroll in graduate school.* Reno, NV: University of Nevada, Reno.

U.S. Department of Education, National Center for Education Statistics (2016). Integrated Postsecondary Education Data System (IPEDS), IPEDS Spring 2016, Human Resources component, Fall Staff section. Retrieved from https://nces.ed.gov/programs/coe/indicator_csc.asp.

CHAPTER 20

GradFIT

Preparing Diverse Undergraduates
for Graduate School

MATTHEW AGUIRRE, MA, TALLINE MARTINS, PH.D.,
and DAVID ZEH, PH.D.

Matthew Aguirre is a graduate assistant for the office of diversity initiatives at the University of Nevada, Reno. He researches and coordinates initiatives that assist in providing a diverse, equitable, and inclusive environment for the University community. Aguirre is currently pursuing a doctoral degree at the University of Nevada, Reno.

Talline Martins is the director of postdoctoral affairs at the University of Nevada, Reno. She develops, oversees, and manages policies relevant to postdoctoral fellows, and serves as an advocate to address issues relevant to postdoctoral fellows. Martins is an experienced educator and higher education administrator with a doctoral degree from the University of Wisconsin, Madison.

David Zeh is the vice provost for graduate education and dean of the Graduate School at the University of Nevada, Reno. He oversees graduate student progress and the rules and regulations governing graduate education. Zeh is an accomplished researcher, professor, and graduate-student advisor with a doctoral degree from the University of Arizona.

Before beginning this chapter, it is important to understand that a graduate student is not a student who graduated with a bachelor's degree. A graduate student is a student who is pursuing a master's or doctoral degree at a higher education institution (HEI). What are graduate degrees and why are they important? In short, these degrees are offered by a graduate school at an HEI. Graduate degrees are obtained by further scholarly research and coursework in specialized fields. According

FIGURE 20.1. Weekly earnings by degrees obtained. (U.S. Department of Labor, 2016)

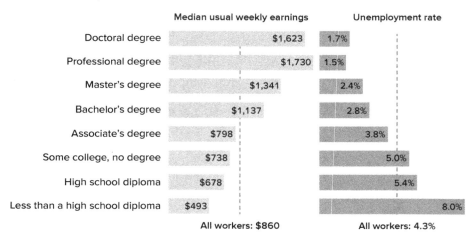

Note: Data are for persons age 25 and over. Earnings are for full-time wage and salary workers.
Source: U.S. Bureau of Labor Statistics, Current Population Survey

to *U.S. News & World Report,* there are six reasons to get a graduate degree (Martin, 2012):

- Personal growth
- Greater employment opportunities
- Greater career advancement
- Financial reward
- Sense of accomplishment
- Greater recognition and credibility

A graduate degree can open more employment opportunities as a bachelor's degree becomes the new minimum education requirement for many jobs posted in the country (Martin, 2012). Graduate degrees can assist in advancing careers to higher roles of leadership (Martin, 2012). Individuals feel a sense of accomplishment upon completing a graduate degree, and at the same time raise their status in society (Martin, 2012). One of the main driving factors for individuals to obtain a graduate degree is the overall financial earnings one can make. On average, a person with a graduate degree can make $17,940 more annually than an individual with a bachelor's degree (U.S. Department of Labor, 2016). In thirty years, that is more than $500,000 of potential earnings an individual can have versus someone with a bachelor degree (U.S. Department of Labor, 2016).

How and where can a graduate degree be obtained? Why are there not more individuals with graduate degrees, if they offer so many benefits? Who does not want all of these advantages? It takes effort, dedication, time, and money to get these prestigious degrees. Now the question becomes, where to start? How does someone learn more about graduate schools and the degrees they offer? What should a person know about applying to a graduate program, and when should the application be completed? What type of degree is best to obtain? How does an individual know if the graduate school is the right choice? Who and where should a person go for assistance with all these questions? The questions can go on, but there is now an answer: GradFIT!

What is GradFIT?

GradFIT is the University of Nevada, Reno's (UNR) five-day intensive academic program for first-generation college students (students whose parent[s] have not obtained at least a bachelor's degree) and for students from historically underrepresented backgrounds who are completing their sophomore or junior year. The program introduces students to the opportunities, challenges, and expectations of graduate school by allowing them to attend academic lectures and workshops, tour labs and facilities, and meet with faculty and graduate students. Students acquire knowledge to create competitive applications and learn about career choices obtainable through a graduate education.

GradFIT's History

In Spring 2014, UNR's vice provost for graduate education and dean of the Graduate School, Dr. David Zeh, and chief diversity officer at the time, Dr. Reginald Chenn Stewart, noticed a disparity in the number of historically underrepresented students in the graduate student population at UNR. This data was obtained from graduate school applications and acceptance offers of domestic students at UNR. Students from historically underrepresented races applied for and accepted offers at drastically unequal rates. GradFIT was created to encourage more

TABLE 20.1. University of Nevada, Reno's Graduate School application/
acceptance by race/ethnicity. (University of Nevada, Reno, 2015)

Race/Ethnicity	Applications (%)	Accepted Offers (%)	U.S. Resident Population, 21 and Older (%)
Hispanic	4.6	5.1	13.9
White	79.2	73.3	67.5
Black	3.4	2.9	11.5
Asian	4.3	4.3	4.9
American Indian/Alaska Native	.6	.8	.6
Pacific Islander	.1	.2	.1
Multiple	7.8	13.3	1.5

students from historically underrepresented races and first-generation college students to apply to graduate school to diversify the graduate student population at UNR. A collaboration began with Nevada State College (NSC) in Henderson, Nevada to meet the needs of their students wanting to pursue a graduate degree but could not continue because NSC does not offer graduate degrees. UNR, seeking a diverse student population, felt NSC's undergraduate student population was the perfect group to pilot the GradFIT program. In the Fall 2013, NSC had 3,394 undergraduate students with 55 percent self-identifying from a historically underrepresented race and 51 percent self-identifying as a first-generation college student (Nevada State College, 2014).

First Year

The GradFIT program became a reality in the Spring 2014 with collaborations from UNR's Graduate School, Office of Diversity Initiatives, and NSC (The Center for Student Cultural Diversity, 2014). GradFIT's first cohort was eight junior-standing undergraduate NSC students from diverse races with interest in pursuing graduate degrees in the fields of biology and psychology. These students self-identified as coming from a historically underrepresented race or a first-generation college student. The program brought these students to UNR's campus for three days at no financial expense to them (The Center for Student Cultural Diversity, 2014). The two collaborating institutions covered the cost of meals, lodging, and transportation. The NSC students attended activities covering topics to prepare them for graduate school. These topics included (The Center for Student Cultural Diversity, 2014):

- Presentation on "Why Graduate School and Why the University of Nevada, Reno."
- Lectures by UNR faculty
- Tour of campus and laboratories
- Workshop on preparing for the Graduate Record Exam
- Workshop on communicating with faculty advisors and writing a personal statement
- Financial aid workshop specific to graduate students
- Panel discussion with graduate students

Because of the positive student feedback from the pilot group of students, GradFIT was deemed a success. Discussions focused on continuing the program annually and expanding the graduate programs, the number of days, and the number of students served. From the eight NSC students, three attended UNR for their graduate studies, and one enrolled in a doctoral program at the University of Nevada, Las Vegas. One student shared their experience with an NSC faculty member on the GradFIT program's impact on their education. Below is an excerpt from their conversation:

> [A] GradFIT participant was working full-time and taking one or two classes a semester and although interested in furthering their education, they had the feeling that graduate school was not something they could do as a nontraditional student. Then they went to GradFIT, and the day after returning from GradFIT, they put in their two-week notice at work and enrolled in school full-time. They have been a powerhouse student ever since, being heavily involved in the academic success center, student government, and more. Now they are graduating with their undergraduate degree and going on to pursue a doctoral degree (Faculty, 2016).

Second Year

Continuing the momentum of the pilot year, GradFIT returned in the spring 2015. The program was expanded from three days to four days to include more content. The number of represented graduate programs and students increased. The participants were in one of three academic groups based on their majors: the life sciences; psychology, behavioral, and social sciences; and the creative and liberal arts. The program accepted students from the following undergraduate majors:

- Animal sciences
- Biology
- English
- Psychology
- Social psychology
- Sociology
- Biological sciences
- Business management and marketing
- Food and nutrition communication
- Rangeland ecology and management
- Social work
- Women studies

GradFIT continued its collaboration with NSC but also included undergraduate students from California State University, Chico; California State University, Sacramento; and UNR. Students of these HEIs were asked to submit an online application and were selected to participate based on grade point average (GPA), class standing, and answers to essay questions asked in the application (Center for Student Cultural Diversity, 2015). Thirty-two students, ranging from sophomore standing to having recently graduated with their bachelor's degree, were accepted. They all self-identified as being first-generation college students or from a historically underrepresented race. GradFIT was again provided at no cost to the students with the HEIs subsidizing the cost of meals, lodging, and transportation.

Various activities and topics included many of the previous cohort's topics with some additions (The Center for Student Cultural Diversity, 2015):

- Presentation on "Why Graduate School and Why the University of Nevada, Reno"
- Lectures by UNR faculty
- Tours of facilities and laboratories by UNR faculty
- Tour of campus and graduate housing

TABLE 20.2 Breakdown of student participants by their respective HEI (Center for Student Cultural Diversity, 2015)

Institution	Number of Students
CSU, Chico	6
CSU, Sacramento	9
Nevada State College	9
University of Nevada, Reno	8
Total	32

- Presentation on "Why Reno Is a Great Place to Live"
- Workshop on preparing for the Graduate Record Exam (GRE)
- Presentations on graduate admissions and assistantships
- Workshop on communicating with faculty and writing a personal statement
- Interactive workshop regarding careers and financial advice
- Tour and information session of the Desert Research Institute
- Trip to and information session on Lake Tahoe
- Panel discussion with graduate students

Once again, because of the positive student feedback from the second cohort, GradFIT was seen as a success. Currently, five of the students from that cohort have pursued a graduate degree, while the others continue to complete their undergraduate degrees.

Third Year

UNR's Graduate School expanded various components of GradFIT in the spring of 2016. The program expanded from four days to five to expand on the current content of the program. Participants were grouped into four categories based on the graduate program in which they were interested:

- Group 1: Biological sciences, genetics, and computer science, and engineering
- Group 2: Public health, medicine, and social work
- Group 3: English, education, sociology, and economics
- Group 4: Psychology, neuroscience, and social psychology

TABLE 20.3. Breakdown of students selected
to participate in the program by institution.

Institution	Number of Students
CSU, Sacramento	9
Nevada State College	11
San Jose State University	1
University of Nevada, Reno	7
Total	28

GradFIT continued its collaboration with NSC and CSU, Sacramento, and included San Jose State University. Students submitted an online application to GradFIT and were selected based on the criteria used in the second year. Twenty-eight students were chosen.

These twenty-eight students ranged from sophomore standing to completing their bachelor's degree and self-identified as a first-generation college student or from a historically underrepresented race. The program was again provided at no cost because of the collaboration of the HEIs subsidizing. The activities and informational sessions covered many topics from the second year, but also included additions:

- Presentation on why graduate school is important and the opportunities a graduate education can afford
- Motivational keynote
- Graduate program application workshop
- Presentation on financial aid
- Presentation on graduate assistantships and fellowships
- Writing a personal statement
- Importance of health and fitness while pursuing a graduate education
- Presentation on the Graduate Student Association's resources
- Lectures by University of Nevada, Reno faculty
- Tours of facilities and laboratories by UNR faculty
- Workshop on preparing for the Graduate Record Exam (GRE)
- Tour, information session, and faculty networking at the Desert Research Institute
- Trip to and information session on Lake Tahoe
- Panel discussion with graduate students
- Forum with University faculty members and graduate students

GradFIT proved to be a success based on data collected from the third cohort. Responses from the participants' initial applications were compared with their responses after GradFIT; this type of analysis was not conducted in previous years. The data showed significant gains in knowledge about admissions requirements, financial aid, GRE, and student life.

The data show more participants considering attending the University of Nevada, Reno for their graduate education (Graph 20.4 & Graph 20.5).

The participants' responses about GradFIT workshops and activities were positive, as shown in graphs 20.6 and 20.7.

Many said GradFIT was inspiring, motivational, informational, welcoming, and supportive. Participants were thankful to be a part of the program.

GradFIT's Future

Because of the success of GradFIT, the program will continue annually basis with plans to expand the number of student participants and graduate programs represented. GradFIT will continue to assist and motivate students from historically underrepresented races and first-generation college students to pursue a graduate degree whether at UNR or another institution of higher education. There is a need for a program such as GradFIT and it will continue to serve students from underrepresented backgrounds until equity and inclusion of all populations exist at the graduate school level.

References

The Center for Student Cultural Diversity. (2014). *Annual report 2014*. University of Nevada, Reno. Retrieved from http://www.unr.edu/Documents/student-services/cultural-diversity/annual-reports/2014%20Annual%20Report%20Final.pdf.

The Center for Student Cultural Diversity. (2015). *Annual report 2015*. University of Nevada, Reno. Retrieved from http://www.unr.edu/Documents/student-services/cultural-diversity/annual-reports/2015_Annual_Report.pdf.

Faculty. (2016). Email exchange. Nevada State College.

Martin, D. (2012). Six reasons why graduate school pays off. *U.S. News & World Report*.

Retrieved from http://www.usnews.com/education/best-graduate-schools/articles/2012/06/29/6-reasons-why-graduate-school-pays-off.

Nevada State College. (2014). Fast Facts. *Nevada State College*.

U.S. Department of Labor. (2016). Earnings and unemployment rates by educational attainment. (2016). Retrieved Sept. 23, 2016, from http://www.bls.gov/emp/ep_chart_001.htm.

FIGURE 20.2. Pre-GradFIT: Application responses.

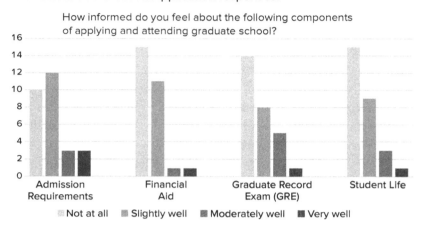

FIGURE 20.3. Post-GradFIT: Evaluation responses.

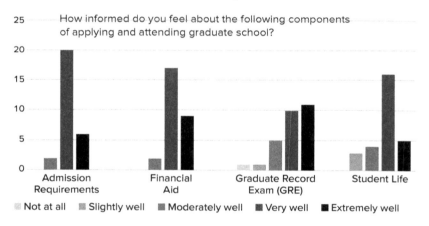

FIGURE 20.4. Pre-GradFIT: Application responses.

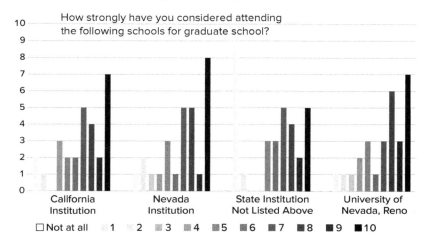

FIGURE 20.5. Post-GradFIT: Evaluation responses.

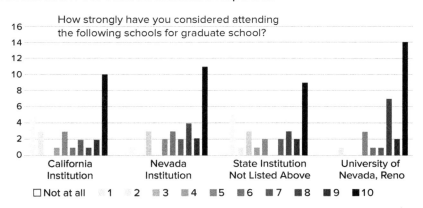

FIGURE 20.6. Participant responses to workshop evaluations.

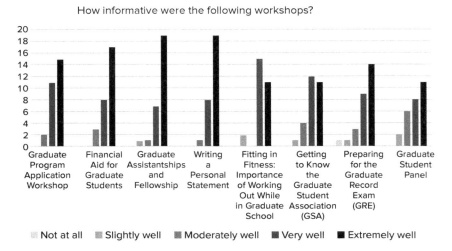

FIGURE 20.7. Participant responses to program evaluations.

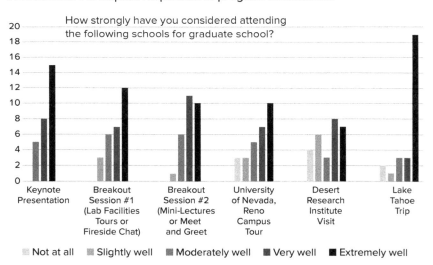

CHAPTER 21

The School of Medicine's Post-Baccaluareate Program

Megan Almansoori, MA

Megan Almansoori is the director of educational outreach and pipeline programs at the University of Nevada, Reno School of Medicine, where she assists all levels of students with preparing for applying to medical school. She has more than twenty years of experience working in education and has focused on supporting students from economically and educationally disadvantaged backgrounds. Almansoori is currently pursuing a Ph.D. in equity and diversity in education at the University of Nevada, Reno.

Program Overview

Nevada is forty-ninth in the country in the number of active patient care physicians per capita. Coupled with the fact that we are only supplying the country with 0.5 percent of its medical school applicants, it becomes clear that we have a dire need to prepare and retain highly qualified physicians who are committed to serving the population of the state. The University of Nevada, Reno School of Medicine (UNR Med) is devoted to improving the health and well-being of all Nevadans and their communities by selecting, training, and supporting physicians who strive to provide the highest quality health care throughout the state.

UNR Med believes that there is no single, correct way to pursue a career in medicine. There are many potential physicians who do not fit the mold of "traditional" premedical students; some had to work to support family members throughout their undergraduate career, some may have decided on medicine later in life, while others may have taken longer to find a support system and reach their academic potential. For these types of students, we have developed the Post-Baccalaureate Program, a structured, one-year certificate program designed for students who need

GPA improvement, Medical College Admission Test (MCAT) preparation, or additional upper-division science coursework to be competitive for medical school admissions. Preference for admittance into the UNR Med Post-Baccalaureate Program is given to Nevada residents who identify as a member of an underserved population in education and/or health care. This includes students who are first-generation, from a low-income household, an underrepresented minority, from rural or urban underserved communities, or are veterans.

History

The Post-Baccalaureate Program began as a way to help students from educationally or medically disadvantaged backgrounds prepare for both the admissions process and the academic rigor of medical school. The program started as a collaboration between UNR Med and the University of Nevada, Reno (UNR) undergraduate campus in the Fall 2010 with a pilot program of six students. Since then, the program has expanded its partnerships to two additional undergraduate institutions: the University of Nevada, Las Vegas (UNLV), and Nevada State College (NSC) in Henderson. It currently enrolls eighteen students through both the regular program track as well as a new, accelerated program for students who have already applied to medical school. To date, the Post-Baccalaureate Program has helped forty-three students complete the program to become better prepared for medical school, and has seen 50 percent accepted to medical school or other health professions programs, while 35 percent are currently applying.

Structure

Students accepted into the Post-Baccalaureate Program take a minimum of thirty-two credits in one academic year in upper-division biology, biochemistry, public health, and other related subjects at their assigned undergraduate institution. The course load and schedule are rigorous. The program is intended to mimic the intensity of medical school to prepare the students for the difficult work ahead. Programs of study are created individually for each student based on their academic needs. Students are also required to attend regular workshops and advising meetings throughout the year as well as take an intensive MCAT preparation course before they take the test in mid-late summer.

Students must achieve a 3.5 overall GPA for the program year and receive an approved MCAT score to complete the program. Students who meet the minimum criteria may apply for early admissions seats with the University of Nevada, Reno School of Medicine in the summer following their program year.

Student Success Stories

Steve, Class of 2013

As immigrants from Colombia and Guatemala, Steve's parents believed that his efforts would be better spent making money immediately in the workforce rather than going to college. He often felt torn between what he was learning in school and what he was hearing at home, causing him to feel isolated in both environments. The mixed messages, however, did not deter Steve from pursuing his own path. He graduated from the University of Nevada, Las Vegas in 2003 with a bachelor's degree in cellular and molecular biology.

After graduation, Steve spent the next nine years of his life volunteering and working in the medical field. His work as a pharmacy technician at University Medical Center in Las Vegas provided him with opportunities to discuss and observe the role of physicians in the hospital, inspiring him to return to school to ultimately become their colleague. In 2012, after nearly a decade of being out of the classroom, Steve entered the Post-Baccalaureate Program to prepare himself for the road to becoming a physician.

Steve's life experience and maturity were major assets to both himself and the rest of his cohort in the Post-Baccalaureate Program. He was an excellent teacher and mentor and continued to provide guidance for students in the following years. In 2013, Steve was accepted to the University of Nevada, Reno School of Medicine where his attributes have continued to serve him.

Cindy, Class of 2014

Cindy grew up in an area of Santa Ana, California, that was overrun by gangs, drugs, teen pregnancies, and high school dropouts. Raised by her single mother, she was often responsible for helping keep her brothers either out of jail or from the grips of a methamphetamine addiction. Despite her barriers, Cindy became the first in her family to go to college, and she completed her bachelor's degree in physiology and neuroscience from the University of California, San Diego in 2012.

With family issues consistently arising during her undergraduate career, it was difficult for Cindy to perform to her true potential. Working as a medical interpreter at a hospital and having helped her brother through his addiction, she knew that she wanted to pursue a career in medicine but recognized that her grades would not make her a competitive candidate. Dealing with the difficulties in her personal life, however, had made Cindy extremely resilient and mature. After graduating from college, she realized that her situation would never change if she continued to let her family's challenges control her path. Rather than let her past determine the future, she chose to persevere and continue to pursue her passion for medicine. The shift in perspective led her to apply to the Post-Baccalaureate Program.

Cindy's drive and maturity served her well in the Post-Baccalaureate Program. Being away from home allowed her to focus on her coursework, and she was able to show what she was capable of in an academic environment. She thrived in her year at UNR, both in her classes and extracurricular activities, which included interpreting and then developing an interpreter-training program for the UNR Med Student Outreach Clinic. When Cindy was accepted to the University of Nevada, Reno, School of Medicine in 2015, it was clear that her choice to persevere had paid off.

Serenity, Class of 2015

Serenity is the second youngest of five children and the first in her family to go to college. Having grown up in a single-parent, low-income household, Serenity did not consider that a college degree was an option for her until high school. Before graduating high school, she became pregnant, but having a child did not deter her from pursuing higher education. In 2014, Serenity graduated from the University of Nevada, Reno with a bachelor's degree in neuroscience.

Navigating both the college environment and motherhood was a major challenge during her undergraduate career. Serenity often had to work two jobs while trying to be successful in her classes and provide the best care for her son. Despite the challenge of balancing family, work, and school, she found the time to co-create and act as the president of UNR's ABLE Women student organization, a community service group which aimed to improve diversity on campus through community service and academic excellence.

Serenity has an ability to take life in stride, a perspective which greatly benefited her throughout college and while in the Post-Baccalaureate Program. She completed the program, and completed it well, in 2015. She was immediately accepted into the University of Nevada, Reno, School of Medicine and is currently studying to graduate with the medical student class of 2020.

Brittiany, Class of 2016

As a first-generation college student, Brittiany had little guidance in pursuing her bachelor's degree. Both of her parents worked to support their family, resulting in Brittiany being raised and cared for by her grandmother. Knowing she would have to help support her family as well, Brittiany worked throughout high school and college while maintaining a full-time course load. It is a testament to her work ethic and drive that she was able to complete two bachelor's degrees by the time she graduated from the University of Nevada, Las Vegas in 2014: she earned a bachelor of science in biological science as well as a bachelor of arts in psychology.

While she was pursuing a bachelor's degree, her grandmother became ill and passed away, leaving Brittiany emotionally devastated and ill-equipped to balance work, her classes, and volunteer and clinical experiences. As a result, her academic performance declined for a few semesters. Because of her unwavering determination, Brittiany recovered quickly and greatly improved her grades during the remaining two years of her undergraduate degree, but not before the slip had taken its toll on her GPA and her feeling that she could be competitive for medical school.

Brittiany entered the UNR Med Post-Baccalaureate Program at the Nevada State College campus in 2015, where she excelled in her coursework and fully utilized opportunities and resources presented to her to continue shadowing and become a leader among her peers. She has successfully balanced her schoolwork and personal life throughout the program, and we fully expect she will continue her success as she begins her course of study with the University of Nevada, Reno School of Medicine's class of 2021.

Our Future

The Post-Baccalaureate Program has goals to broaden its reach across Nevada. We have a large, medically underserved population in the rural areas of the state and not enough health professionals with ties to these high-needs communities. In the coming years, our goal is to increase support for rural students interested in pursuing a career in medicine.

References

Association of American Medical Colleges (2015). 2015 State physician workforce data book. Available from http://members.aamc.org/eweb/upload/2015StateData-Book%20(revised).pdf

Association of American Medical Colleges. (2016). Table A-1: U.S. medical school applications and matriculants by school, state of legal residence, and sex, 2015–2016 [Data file]. Retrieved from https://www.aamc.org/data/facts/applicantmatriculant/

The Future of Federally Funded Programs Serving First-Generation and Low-Income Students

MARITZA MACHADO-WILLIAMS, PH.D.

Maritza Machado-Williams serves as the executive director of the Academic and Opportunity Support Programs office, which houses the McNair Scholars, GEAR UP, TRiO Scholars, Nevada First in the Pack, and three Upward Bound programs. Her research interest is in issues impacting college access and achievement of first-generation, low-income, and international students as well as first and second language acquisition and learning theory. Machado-Williams has a Ph.D. in curriculum and instruction from the University of Kansas.

Inequality of opportunity for higher education is a brutal fact of life in the United States. In 2015, a child born into a family with an income in the top quartile of family incomes (above \$120,000) had about 58 percent chance of completing degree by age twenty-four. If the child was born into the bottom quartile of family income (\$38,000), then the student had a 12 percent chance of completing a degree by age twenty-four. (Mortenson, 2017, p.1)

Many research studies have examined the academic achievement gaps of students who come from low-income families, are first generation in their family to go to college, or are classified as underrepresented in higher education (Edmonson, Fisher, & Christensen, 2003; Hsuch & Yoshikawa, 2007; Mitchem & Becker, 2016; Mortenson 2017; Striplin, 1999). Many others explore the intersection of those factors as powerful deterrents that have to be confronted in and outside the classroom through tutoring, mentoring, the development of learning communities, advising, and classes specifically designed to address the needs of the population (Thayer, 2000; Ayala & Striplen, 2002).

Similarly, current literature on college access, progression, and completion have documented the effectiveness of specific academic support programs designed to provide comprehensive academic services to the above-mentioned populations. Those studies have concluded that there is evidence of their significant impact on access to postsecondary education and college graduation (Gullatt & Jan, 2003). More specifically, programs such as the Gaining Early Awareness and Readiness for Undergraduate Programs (GEAR UP) support federal goals of secondary school completion, college preparation, college enrollment, undergraduate completion, and graduate school preparation of first-generation and low-income students as well as of veterans, students with disabilities, and displaced workers.

A six-year longitudinal study conducted by the Policy and Program Studies Services of the United States Department of Education in 2010, for instance, seems to confirm such findings. This time, the most significant conclusions of the *National Evaluation of Student Support Services: Examination of Student Outcomes After Six Years* study are the following:

- There is a correlation between academic support services provided through the Student Support Services (TRiO) program and the improvement of student academic outcome, particularly in the first year of college.
- Support services received during the first year of college continue to have an impact after the freshman year and show a stronger relationship to long-term outcomes beyond the first year.
- A group of specific services provided by Student Support Services program (peer tutoring, labs, workshops, services for students with disabilities, counseling, field trips or cultural enrichment, referrals to outside resources, services for those with limited English ability, college reentrance counseling, and continued contacts with the program) as well as the format used to deliver those services ("home based" and "blended" programs) seem to be closely related to improved students' outcomes.
- Services received after the freshman year were more effective in predicting long-term outcomes. Further, depending on the methodology used by the studies, the benefits of the services provided by

the Student Support Services programs seem to be underestimated by contemporary research.

Equally important are two of the findings of a similar study focused on services offered by the Upward Bound program, one of the "oldest continually-operating college access programs" (Mitchem & Becker, 2016, p. 3). This research suggests that:

- Upward Bound has a substantial impact on high school and post-secondary outcomes for students who have lower academic expectations and who do not expect at the time of application to participate in the program to earn a bachelor's degree.
- Staying in Upward Bound for longer periods of time increases the chances of students attending postsecondary institutions. (U.S. Department of Education, 2004).

Although the same study presents other inconclusive findings, local data obtained for the purpose of reporting to the United States Department of Education in 2015–2016 highlighted these and other positive outcomes at the University of Nevada, Reno when Upward Bound performance goals exceeded expectations in several areas. Those areas included math and reading proficiency levels, GPA, high school retention, graduation with a regular high school diploma, and enrollment in institutions of postsecondary education the fall after graduation from high school. These and other research outcomes document the impact of these programs that, although embedded in colleges, universities, and not-for profit organizations, receive federal funding and oversight through the United States Department of Education Office of Postsecondary Education.

However, because of changing practices, there is a critical need to examine past and present achievements to better serve the student population and maximize the benefits of the models.

By definition, federal programs are dependent on federal resources, and thus subject to the unforeseeable and unpredictable shifts in public policy, budget appropriations, and specific administrations' goals. Consequently, GEAR UP and TRiO administrators are often skeptical of the future of the programs:

I wish I had a better feeling for what the future of the TRiO/ GEAR UP programs holds, but with the current political climate in Washington, D.C., a future for these programs is uncertain. Prior administrations have tried to eliminate funding for TRiO/GEAR UP, but I always trusted that we would have funding. Yet, under the Trump administration, and for the first time in my twenty years working with TRiO programs, I am fearful of not being funded. And if funding is pulled, my current institution does not have the funds to take over the services that we currently provide. The program would fold, and the special populations we serve would no longer have an advocate for them on campus.

—Director of a TRiO program in the Midwest
(personal communication, July 17, 2017.)

At one time or another, every director of a federally funded program like GEAR UP thinks about that question. What is the future of my program? We know the difference we make on the life of low-income and first gen students and their families. Our college appreciates our work and how our work contributes to the retention and graduation strategic goals of the institution, but what if? We have to think strategically and focus on how our program will evolve and grow rather than thinking about the opposite. I have to say, that with the current political climate, I spent more time thinking about survival than about growth. I have been with GEAR UP since 1999 serving students and families from the inner city and the suburbs and have never felt this way until now. Honestly, I think we will be lucky if we survive the next four or eight years. I guess we'll have to fight harder for our programs and our students. Nevertheless, I want to remain optimistic that my university will adapt some if not all of our best practices. We consistently exceed graduation rates of the school district and enrollment rates into post-secondary.

—Director of a GEAR UP program on the West Coast
(personal communication, July 18. 2017.)

The sentiments expressed by these administrators suggest that institutions and organizations should consider changing their practices, aiming to replicate their success but with nonfederal forms of funding. The task is challenging but critical. Currently, TRiO programs alone serve 790,000 participants, and colleges have documented growing number of students who qualify for services (Council for Opportunity in Education, 2017). A few examples of integrated initiatives addressing the needs of first-generation, low-income students with institutional resources: First Scholars, a program funded by the Souder Foundation, serving students at six universities; the University of Washington Dream Project partnering with multiple local and national organizations to increase access to higher education; the First-Generation Student Success Program hosted by the University of La Verne (CA) Center for Multicultural Services, promoting diversity, educational opportunity, and success; the First Graduate, a San Francisco-based college-success program offering college and career coaching in a ten-year commitment to 450 first-generation students; and the Nevada First in the Pack, funded by the University of Nevada, Reno, serving 100 first-generation freshmen. The commitment of these institutions to educational opportunity and equity is robust and capable of withstanding the ever-changing political climate of the country while addressing issues specific to each institution and its population, leveraging local resources, and developing a network of support for all students. Further, Mitchem and Becker (2016) assert that institutions and educational leaders must think strategically and leverage college access programs to advance the institution's short- and long-term goals based on what they describe as four core principles:

- Longevity: An institutional commitment is needed to sustain the work of the program as long as the need exists. This includes providing financial and in-kind resources to promote continuity of services, short-term interventions, and long-term goals.
- Cultural competence: The ability to understand and effectively communicate with students, faculty, and administrators across cultures is imperative. Clearly, staff members need to understand and relate to the cultures of the students they serve. But to be effective, college access programs need staff members who also understand the culture of higher education in general and the unique culture of their institution specifically.

- Asset leveraging: The work of programs such as TRiO and GEAR UP is fully aligned with the goals of institutions seeking to promote academic success and college completion. This concerted effort becomes an asset that advances the mission of the institution and promotes the growth of the organization.
- Strategic organization positioning—networking: A strong professional relationship with faculty, researchers, and administrators is paramount to the success of program participants, but a strong relationship with the grants, development, marketing, and governmental relation offices is critical to ensure the integrity of the program.

The critical and multilayer role of programs being independently established based on the long-standing experience of TRiO and GEAR UP programs cannot be overstated. But perhaps the words of Maureen Hoyler (2014), president of the Council for Opportunity in Education (COE), before the U.S. Senate Committee on Health, Education, Labor, and Pensions, can underline their importance and her vision for their future:

> Just as student financial assistance for low-income students requires a package made up of grants, loans and work-study support most often from federal, state and institutional sources, state, institutional and private support for college access and success programming should be encouraged. Privately funded college access and success partners are working collaboratively with TRiO in many cities and states including Colorado, Connecticut, Kentucky, and Pennsylvania. COE has introduced one such model with support from the GE Foundation. Any barriers to collaboration among such programs should be removed, and where possible vehicles should be made available to introduce more broadly in institutions, agencies and schools the practices first utilized in TRiO and GEAR UP.

References

Ayala, C. & Striplen. (2002). A career introduction model for first-generation college freshmen students. In E. G. Walz, R. Knowdell, & C. Kirkman (Eds.). *Thriving in Challenging and Uncertain Times* (pp. 57–62). Greensboro, NC: ERIC Clearinghouse on Counseling and Student Services.

Bradford, C. W. (2010). U.S. Department of Education, Office of Planning, Evaluation and Policy Development, Policy and Program Studies Service, National Evaluation of Student Support Services: Examination of student outcomes after six years, Washington, D.C. Retrieved from http://www.ed.gov/about/offices/list/opepd/ppss/reports.html.

Council for Opportunity in Education (2017). *Resources.* Retrieved August 8, 2017 from www.coenet.org/TRiO.shtml.

Edmonson, S., Fisher, A., & Christensen, J. (2003). Project CONNECT: A University's effort to close the gaps (ERIC Ed477438). Paper presented at the Annual Meeting of the American Educational Research Association (Chicago, IL, April 21–25, 2003).

Gullatt, Y. & Wendy J. (2003). How do precollegiate academic outreach programs impact college-going among underrepresented students? Washington, DC: Pathways to College Network Clearinghouse.

Mitchem, A., & Becker, J. (2016). Making college access a priority at four-year colleges and universities. *Lessons from the go college program, 2.* Retrieved from http://www.coenet.org/files/publications-Lessons_from_the_GO_College_Program_April_2016.pdf.

Mortenson, T. (2017–2). Poverty and inequality: family and community life. *Postsecondary Education Opportunity, 288(2).*

Striplin, J. (1999, June). Facilitating transfer for First-Generation Community College Students. *ERIC Digest.* Retrieved from http//www.eric.ed.gov.

Thayer, P. B. (2000, May). Retention of students from first-generation and low income backgrounds. *Opportunity Outlook*, 2–8.

U.S. Department of Education Office of the Under Secretary. (2004). *The impacts of regular upward bound: Results from the third follow-up data collection.* (Mathematica Policy Research, Inc.). Washington, D.C.: Myers, D., Olsen, R., Seftor, N., Young, J., Tuttle, C. Retrieved from https://www2.ed.gov/rschstat/eval/highered/upward/upward-3rd-report.pdf.

U.S. Senate Committee on Health, Education, Labor and Pensions. (2014). *Strengthening Federal Access Programs to Meet 21st Century Needs: A Look at TRiO and GEAR UP.* By M. Hoyler. Retrieved from https://www.help.senate.gov/imo/media/doc/Hoyler.pdf.

Why We Did This
and What You Can Do

We wrote this book to share our programs and research with all of you who share a passion for helping students who may need an extra bit of support on their way to college and during their college experience. The University of Nevada, Reno is an institution that has seen remarkable growth in the last twenty-five years. From a student population of about 11,000 to almost 22,000, students of color have increased from approximately 8 percent of the total student body to more than 40 percent. What has not changed is the percentage of first-generation students as measured by the CIRP (UCLA Cooperative Institutional Research Project) that has been administered regularly over a forty-year period. At over 40 percent, the actual number has increased as enrollment has increased.

Our programs have been implemented with very few resources. Take a look at what you are doing. How can you package what you are doing currently into a program? How can it be branded so that students are aware of your efforts? What assessment measures will help you determine if you are making a meaningful impact? What impact is meaningful in your situational context? Be creative in your thinking and have the courage to do what needs to be done. Remember that you don't need permission to do what is right!

The following items highlight the ways in which the University of Nevada, Reno implemented successful programs and service to support our underrepresented students. We hope that these takeaways prove useful in your venture to serve your student population.

The College Knowledge Gap

- Identify what college knowledge is needed to make recruitment efforts relevant to your populations.
- Assess the college knowledge gaps among existing college student populations.
- Develop mechanisms such as definition campaigns and higher education glossaries to educate those with college knowledge gaps

Dean's Future Scholars

- Focus on creating a comprehensive bridge program to college and career by establishing your program in an academic college.
- Utilize student development theory to recognize the value of students being served and their potential as future proponents of your program.
- Build a partnership with academic faculty to access existing knowledge and research.

Upward Bound

- Explore grant opportunities for college preparatory programs, such as Upward Bound and Upward Bound Math & Science.
- Apply for experimental grants through the U.S. Department of Education, as they become available.
- Do not be confined by the boundaries of physical space and offices, get creative to maximize the grants you do have.

Wolf Pack First

- Identify barriers that prevent students from applying for admission, through partnerships with your Registrar, such as the non-refundable application fee, early admission deposits, and language barriers.
- To serve those who are underrepresented, you must meet them in their communities, remembering that for most underrepresented or first-generation students, college choice is a family decision, not an individual decision.
- Provide intentional and intrusive support through the admissions and new-student process.

Pipeline Programs for Students of Color

- Encourage early college participation through strong working relationships with your local school districts.
- Consider signing a memorandum of understanding to promote dual credit options and pathways that complement a student's required high school curriculum.
- Maintain consistent communication with prospective scholars and connect them with academic colleagues to introduce opportunities.

Recruiting and Retaining Transfer Students

- Establish relationships with local community colleges that create an ease of information to prospective transfer students.
- Support the development of transfer agreements among local institutions to ensure transfer credit articulation and promote degree completion.
- Launch a peer mentorship program to support new transfer students in acclimating to your institution.

Financial Aid and Scholarships

- Through partnerships with academic advisors communicate financial aid as a tool for completion.
- Implement a degree completion initiative such as 30-to-Complete, and use institutional aid as incentive to complete, when applicable.
- Research sources of nonfederal aid for non-FAFSA eligible individuals and educate admissions recruiters on its availability.

Financial Literacy

- Connect with the SALT money program for easy access to existing resources.
- Utilize peer coaching to empower student financial decision making.
- Explore private partnerships and grant opportunities to promote financial literacy.

Advanced Registration

- Build relationships with academic advisors and the registrar to provide early enrollment to new freshmen students.
- Cultivate academic advising plans for four-year enrollment to degree completion.
- Partner with Complete College America's Momentum Year initiative for access to other institution success mechanisms.

NevadaFIT

- Through the involvement and feedback of academic faculty, identify academic challenges for first-year students.
- Create a targeted academic boot camp program that is specific to each academic college's expectations.
- Engage upperclassmen in the boot camp to mentor and welcome students with shared experiences.

TRiO Scholars

- Utilize peer-mentorship to retain both mentors and mentees.
- Provide an inviting physical space for students.
- Offer academic support through tutoring and campus resource partnerships.

First in the Pack

- Collaborate with departments across campus to maximize efforts and inclusion of first-generation students.
- Maximize resources by partnering with community businesses for funding and experiential opportunities.
- Deliver academic and financial aid guidance through one-on-one meetings to support retention among first-generation students.

Golden Scholars

- Implement a strengths-based academic advising model.
- Partner with student support programs to identify underrepresented students in your college.
- Include academic faculty in development initiatives, such as an etiquette dinner.

Honors Program

- Ensure your learning opportunities are both cocurricular and engaging.
- Create residential living learning communities for program participants.
- Promote opportunities for undergraduate research through faculty mentors.

Supporting LGBTQIA+ Students

- Establish a university-wide task force to ensure consistent communication and efforts to address concerns.
- Expand outside of your division to train allies of the LGBTQIA+ community—students seeing their professors and instructors as allies result in welcoming classroom environment.
- Recognize that cultural paradigm shifts require time and dedication; small successes lead to larger, positive impacts.

Veterans and Assistive Technology

- Adjust thinking models to a framework of universal design.
- Structure your software acquisition process to include product accessibility testing.
- Request VPATs on all new electronic products being acquired by the institution.

Student Conduct

- Form a Student Intervention Team (SIT) to support students in crisis.
- Explore ways your student conduct office can engage in preventative and proactive efforts rather than just reactionary programs.
- Make conduct and mediation relevant to the students of today.

McNair Scholars

- Pursue TRiO McNair grants or use the program as a model to develop your own.
- Seek out faculty mentors to promote undergraduate research and graduate education.

- Familiarize students to graduate programs through college visits.

GradFIT

- Develop programs that introduce underrepresented undergraduate students to the possibility of graduate programs.
- Create a graduate degree-seeking culture by including institutional, local, and regional graduate program opportunities.
- Prepare students interested in pursuing a graduate degree though an intensive training program.

The School of Medicine's Post-Bac Program

- Introduce undergraduate students to medical professions through pipeline programs.
- Establish concurrent baccalaureate programs that complement existing academic degrees.
- Through relationships with economic development authorities, identify the current and future unmet demands of medical profession in your region.

The Future of Federally Funded Programs

- Stay informed on political topics in higher education and the greater community.
- Seek new opportunities and constantly evaluate current programs.
- Involve the content experts, your students, into the development of your programs and services.

Acknowledgments

MELISA CHOROSZY, PH.D.

We have affectionately referred to this undertaking as "The Book." I came up with the idea of this "book," but my colleagues made it happen. I did what I do best. I came up with the rationale, the framework, pulled people together, and gave them assignments. And, much to my surprise, they did it! I would like to thank first the key individuals who helped us assemble this work.

Reema Naik jumped in and served as our first editor. This was a challenging task, given the heterogeneity of styles and topics. She infused transitions, ensured consistency in the use of various phrases and abbreviations, and made it a coherent document.

Dr. Rita Laden, emeritus associate vice president for student services, served as our next editor and pointed out all that we had missed. Her penchant for detail and accuracy along with her red pen helped us get closer to publication.

Dr. Shannon Ellis, vice president for student services served as our last editor. She added the final touches that only she would be able to do.

The faculty who authored this collection represented many programs and initiatives across campus. They carved out time to reflect, write, and explore. Many thanks to: Desirae Acosta, MA; Dawn Aeschlimann, MA; Matthew Aguirre; Megan Almansoori; James Beattie, Ph.D.; Terina Caserto, MA; Christina Y. Cho, Ph.D.; Kari Emm, MA; Perry Fittrer, Ph.D.; Lourdes Gonzalez, MA; Geoffrey Green, MA; Mary Heid; Erick Hendrixson; Ellen Houston, MA; Jennifer Lowman, Ph.D.; Maritza Machado-Williams, Ph.D.; Lisa Maletsky, MPH; Carolina Martinez, MA; Talline Martins; Pat Miltenberger, Ph.D.; Quentin Owens, EdM; José Quiroga, MA; Selene Rangel, MA; Matt Smith, Ph.D.; Kim Thomas, JD; Heather Turk, Ph.D.; Tamara M. Valentine, Ph.D.; Daniel Valle, Ph.D.; and David Zeh, Ph.D.

Most important of all, I would like to thank the students who gave us their time and stories. Supporting student success through access and opportunity is what motivated us to write this book. Thank you: Gemma Beltran, BS in biology, BA in spanish (2017); Liliana Davalos, BS in biology (2015), masters in public health (2017); Maria Lee-Camargo, BA in psychology (2015); and Ivón Padilla-Rodríguez, BA in history and philosophy (2015).

Index

About the Editors

Melisa Choroszy, Ph.D.

Melisa N. Choroszy, Ph.D., is the associate vice president for enrollment services at the University of Nevada, Reno where she oversees the offices of Admissions and Records, Financial Aid and Scholarships, Office for Prospective Students, Office of International Students and Scholars, the Disability Resource Center, Academic and Opportunity Support Programs, Veteran Services, and athletic eligibility. She earned a bachelor's degree in comparative literature from Brandeis University followed by a master's degree in education at Tufts University. She obtained post-master's degree graduate certificates in special education and reading from Bridgewater State University and Lesley College. She earned a Ph.D. in elementary education with a focus on reading, language, and mathematics education as well as a minor in school administration from the University of Arizona.

Theo Meek, MA

Theo Meek is a scholar-practitioner at the University of Nevada, Reno. In his currently role as director of advising for the University's Advising Center, he works with interdisciplinary student populations. His research interest is in the disparity amongst college preparation for first-generation college students as well as gateway course policy and development. Meek is pursuing a Ph.D. in public policy at the University of Nevada, Reno.